The USNA 12

Published by Community Christian Ministries
P.O. Box 9754, Moscow, Idaho 83843
208.883.0997 | www.ccmbooks.org

Jim Wilson (editor), *The USNA 12*, First edition, revised

Cover and interior design by Valerie Anne Bost.
Cover photo: U.S. Naval Academy Chapel Dome, © 2016 Horace and Mae Photography,
horaceandmae.com. Used by permission.

Printed in the United States of America.

17 18 19 20 21 22 23 24   10 9 8 7 6 5 4 3 2

The  USNA 2

*Following Christ in the Academy,
the Navy, and Beyond*

EDITED BY JIM WILSON

COMMUNITY
CHRISTIAN
MINISTRIES
MOSCOW, IDAHO
www.ccmbooks.org

I may not always trace the onward course my ship must take,
But looking backward, I behold afar its shining wake,
Illumined with God's light of love, and so onward I go,
In perfect trust that He who holds the helm the course must know.

—*Anonymous*

CONTENTS

FOREWORD

This small book is written primarily for midshipmen at the United States Naval Academy. As of 2016, these midshipmen number over 4,500. They are disciplined and very smart. The Naval Academy ranks number six in engineering among undergraduate colleges in the United States. The dropout rate is very small.

After commissioning in the U.S. Navy and Marine Corps, Naval Academy graduates become highly proficient in several fields. If you want to get a look at their skills, visit an aircraft carrier during air operations or an attack submarine under the polar ice for three months.

Some graduates stay in the Navy for decades until gaining a high rank or retiring. Others leave the service earlier, and, because of their education, experience, leadership, and intelligence, you will find them in leadership in skilled civilian professions such as engineering, law, or medicine. If you add to these accomplishments the joy, love, peace, and integrity of being a Christian, you will find lives like the ones in the following short autobiographies.

The main objective of this book is to exalt the Lord Jesus Christ. The second objective is to help midshipmen come to the Father through the Son. The book is about the changes in people's lives. The real result of these changes is everlasting life. A third objective is to encourage other Christians to write their testimonies and distribute them.

The New Testament tells us of the conversion of Saul of Tarsus, one of the foremost anti-Christians of his time. There is no doubt that he is one of the greatest Christians in his conversion, his life, and his death.

Saul's story is recorded three times in Acts. I have included two of the accounts in this book. Acts 9 records Saul's conversion. Acts 22 is his testimony before a crowd of Jews while he was a Roman prisoner—a testimony that caused a riot. Acts 26 is his testimony before Festus and Agrippa after he had been in prison for two years following his appeal to Caesar. I mention these accounts to point out the importance of testimony in evangelism.

The common theme in this book is that each of the men in the following stories had his life changed when he was introduced to the Father through the Son. I know each of these men and have stayed in touch with them over the years. Two of us are from the class of 1950, one from the class of 1958, and the rest are from the class of 1962. Because I was their teacher, it is natural that my name should show up in their testimonies. Where I thought the praise of me was too much, I removed it.

A.J. Egerton passed away before this book was written; I have included his story in an appendix. When the class of '62 came to the Naval Academy in 1958, the ensign in charge of midshipmen, Otto Helweg, had been a Christian one year. We were not able to get his testimony for the first printing of *The USNA 12* and shared two messages from him in an appendix in lieu of it. We have received good feedback on those messages and are including them again in this revision. After each testimony, with the exception of Lee Bendell's, A.J. Egerton's, and Otto Helweg's, there is information on how to contact the author.

Enjoy the read.

JIM WILSON

Moscow, Idaho, February 2017

INTRODUCTION

SAUL'S CONVERSION (ACTS 9:1–19)

Meanwhile, Saul was still breathing out murderous threats against the Lord's disciples. He went to the high priest and asked him for letters to the synagogues in Damascus, so that if he found any there who belonged to the Way, whether men or women, he might take them as prisoners to Jerusalem. As he neared Damascus on his journey, suddenly a light from heaven flashed around him. He fell to the ground and heard a voice say to him, "Saul, Saul, why do you persecute me?"

"Who are you, Lord?" Saul asked.

"I am Jesus, whom you are persecuting," he replied. "Now get up and go into the city, and you will be told what you must do."

The men traveling with Saul stood there speechless; they heard the sound but did not see anyone. Saul got up from the ground, but when he opened his eyes he could see nothing. So they led him by the hand into Damascus. For three days he was blind, and did not eat or drink anything.

In Damascus there was a disciple named Ananias. The Lord called to him in a vision, "Ananias!"

"Yes, Lord," he answered.

The Lord told him, "Go to the house of Judas on Straight Street and ask for a man from Tarsus named Saul, for he is praying. In a vision he has seen a man named Ananias come and place his hands on him to restore his sight."

"Lord," Ananias answered, "I have heard many reports about this man and all the harm he has done to your holy people in Jerusalem. And he has come here with authority from the chief priests to arrest all who call on your name."

But the Lord said to Ananias, "Go! This man is my chosen instrument to proclaim my name to the Gentiles and their kings and to the people of Israel. I will show him how much he must suffer for my name."

Then Ananias went to the house and entered it. Placing his hands on Saul, he said, "Brother Saul, the Lord—Jesus, who appeared to you on the road as you were coming here—has sent me so that you may see again and be filled with the Holy Spirit." Immediately, something like scales fell from Saul's eyes, and he could see again. He got up and was baptized, and after taking some food, he regained his strength.

Paul Before Agrippa (Acts 26)

Then Agrippa said to Paul, "You have permission to speak for yourself."

So Paul motioned with his hand and began his defense: "King Agrippa, I consider myself fortunate to stand before you today as I make my defense against all the accusations of the Jews, and especially so because you are well acquainted with all the Jewish customs and controversies. Therefore, I beg you to listen to me patiently.

"The Jewish people all know the way I have lived ever since I was a child, from the beginning of my life in my own country, and also in Jerusalem. They have known me for a long time and can testify, if they are willing, that I conformed to the strictest sect of our religion, living as a Pharisee. And now it is because of my hope in what God has promised our ancestors that I am on trial today. This is the promise our twelve tribes are hoping to see fulfilled as they earnestly serve God day and night. King Agrippa, it is because of this hope that these Jews are accusing me. Why should any of you consider it incredible that God raises the dead?

"I too was convinced that I ought to do all that was possible to oppose the name of Jesus of Nazareth. And that is just what I did in Jerusalem. On the authority of the chief priests I put many of the Lord's people in prison, and when they were put to death, I cast my vote against them. Many a time I went from one synagogue to another to have them punished, and I tried to force them to blaspheme. I was so obsessed with persecuting them that I even hunted them down in foreign cities.

"On one of these journeys I was going to Damascus with the authority and commission of the chief priests. About noon, King Agrippa, as I was on the road, I saw a light from heaven, brighter than the sun, blazing around me and my companions. We all fell to the ground, and I heard a voice saying to me in Aramaic,

"'Saul, Saul, why do you persecute me? It is hard for you to kick against the goads.'

"Then I asked, 'Who are you, Lord?'

"'I am Jesus, whom you are persecuting,' the Lord replied. 'Now get up and stand on your feet. I have appeared to you to appoint you as a servant and as a witness of what you have seen and will see of me. I will rescue you from your own people and from the Gentiles. I am sending you to them to open their eyes and turn them from darkness to light, and from the power of Satan to God, so that they may receive forgiveness of sins and a place among those who are sanctified by faith in me.'

"So then, King Agrippa, I was not disobedient to the vision from heaven. First to those in Damascus, then to those in Jerusalem and in all Judea, and then to the Gentiles, I preached that they should repent and turn to God and demonstrate their repentance by their deeds. That is why some Jews seized me in the temple courts and tried to kill me. But God has helped me to this very day; so I stand here and testify to small and great alike. I am saying nothing beyond what the prophets and Moses said would happen—that the Messiah would suffer and, as the first to rise from the dead, would bring the message of light to his own people and to the Gentiles."

At this point Festus interrupted Paul's defense. "You are out of your mind, Paul!" he shouted. "Your great learning is driving you insane."

"I am not insane, most excellent Festus," Paul replied. "What I am saying is true and reasonable. The king is familiar with these things, and I can speak freely to him. I am convinced that none of this has escaped his notice, because it was not done in a corner. King Agrippa, do you believe the prophets? I know you do."

Then Agrippa said to Paul, "Do you think that in such a short time you can persuade me to be a Christian?"

Paul replied, "Short time or long—I pray to God that not only you but all who are listening to me today may become what I am, except for these chains."

The king rose, and with him the governor and Bernice and those sitting with them. After they left the room, they began saying to one another, "This man is not doing anything that deserves death or imprisonment."

Agrippa said to Festus, "This man could have been set free if he had not appealed to Caesar."

A TESTIMONY
TO GOD'S GRACE

Larry Yandell, USNA Class of '62

was born in 1940 to loving parents that were committed Christians. Like many people, I grew up in a church environment filled with religious activity. Because of this exposure, from my early days I had a mental picture that I was a Christian. In reality, although I knew all the right words, memorized Scripture, and could give right responses to religious questions, I had not made a personal commitment to Jesus Christ and was not a Christian. I made a profession of faith and was baptized when I was nine years old, but my life did not reflect a changed heart. I was proud (always looking to further myself, even at the expense of others), ambitious, and easily angered. There was nothing in my life that would have prompted anyone to consider me a Christian.

During my difficult first year at the Naval Academy, while on my own for the first time, I came to the realization that my religious background was meaningless and that my professed faith was an empty shell. During this period of doubt, I visited the Christian bookstore in Annapolis (because it seemed like the right thing to do) and was invited by Jim Wilson, the Officers' Christian Union representative, to attend a Christian retreat during the term break weekend in January 1959. Because I had nothing planned, it seemed like the right (religious) thing to do, so I agreed to go.

I look back now and recognize that God had ordained to do a marvelous thing in my heart that weekend, to remove the "blinders" and cause me to understand my lost condition apart from Him. At the retreat, I met several Christian midshipmen who seemed to have a warm, personal relationship with Jesus that I had never experienced. It's an embarrassing element of my testimony that I had probably heard the Gospel numerous times during my upbringing without result, but God used this retreat to reach my hardened heart.

Speaking from the book of Hebrews, a gentleman named Don Hullin talked about "a red carpet that ushers us into the presence of God" and that this "red carpet is the blood of Jesus Christ." That picture resonated with me, causing me to recognize that I had no personal relationship with Christ, despite all the "head knowledge" I had accumulated. Don made it clear that as a sinner I was incapable of working my way into a right relationship with God; that only by confessing my sin and through faith in Jesus Christ could I be sure of eternal life. I made the decision to do that and placed my faith in Jesus that weekend.

What a relief to know that the experience was real and that something in me was different! It was not a powerful, emotional experience—rather a deep-seated assurance of having a right standing before God. This freed me from all the mental "bookkeeping" that I had been using to determine if I was doing enough to get to heaven. The reality sunk in: by His death on the cross, Christ had paid the penalty for my sins and invited me to walk that "red carpet" into the presence of the Father.

God has blessed me greatly since that time of decision. The Bible suddenly became clear and relevant in my life, the Spirit confirmed to my spirit that I was a child of God, and I developed a love for the brethren that I had not experienced before. Even fifty years later, the Christian bonds I formed at the Naval Academy are still some of the strongest, most enduring friendships I have. God has given me a marvelous wife who loves the Lord. Judy has a Christian bent for service and a heart for prayer and is a great encourager in my Christian walk. The Lord has opened doors to enable me to teach Bible classes and a Christian Worldview class to high school students. Life has taken a wonderful turn for the better since that decision at the retreat in 1959. Even during times of hardship and disappointment, we rest on God's sovereignty and take comfort that He is in control of every circumstance for our good and His glory.

Our prayer is to be able to look back and see a life that is reflective of the last verse of the old hymn that goes...

When He shall come with trumpet sound,
Oh may I then in Him be found;
Dressed in His righteousness alone,
Faultless to stand before the throne.

…and to be able to say with truth and conviction the opening
line of the chorus: "On Christ the solid rock I stand." We continually thank God for His providential care and look forward
with assurance to what He will accomplish in the future.

Larry Yandell can be contacted at larryyandell@BWDMAIL.net.

MY TESTIMONY TO FAITH IN JESUS CHRIST

Captain Robert P. Greenman, US Navy (Retired),
USNA Class of '62

The purpose of this testimony is to honor Jesus Christ and to be an encouragement to others. It describes the journey—His *gift* to me as I "work out my salvation"—I lived out in real life. Fortunately, God gave me my precious wife, Margie, to whom, after Jesus, I owe everything.

I was born in 1940, baptized and brought up in the Episcopal Church. My mother was a godly woman who took us to church regularly and consistently lived her faith in Jesus. However, I essentially did what I was told (went through all the motions) but made no real commitment to God nor had a personal relationship with Him.

I became a midshipman at the U.S. Naval Academy with the class of 1962. In my junior year, a good friend with whom I rowed crew told me about his faith in Jesus. I respected him, knew there was something different about him, and appreciated his sharing, but did nothing more.

In my senior year, I was having difficulties with a relationship with a girl. More fundamentally, though, I was confused, lacked purpose and perspective, questioned why I was at the Academy, and was uneasy about my future. In February 1962, my roommate put me in contact with Jim Wilson, USNA '50, who was the local representative for the Officers' Christian Fellowship and ran a Christian bookstore in Annapolis. Using the Bible, he explained the plan of salvation to me in a way I had not understood before, and the Holy Spirit did a work in me to receive it. Jim made me see that I was trying to run my own life independent of God, but that God had saved me and wanted to restore our relationship. He helped me understand that I needed to repent of my sins and accept Jesus, God's Son, as my personal Savior. I went back to my room and prayed, asking God to forgive me and for Jesus to come into my life. God made me a new creature, and my relationship with Jesus became personal and life-changing. Like the father in the Parable of the Prodigal Son, Jesus came running towards me, and I became His.

Very shortly, I knew something had happened. I had a peace and perspective I had been missing. The Bible became very interesting and important to me, and I gravitated to the company of midshipmen who had a similar faith. God took away my desire to talk dirty, even though

I had not asked Him to do this because it had contributed to my popularity (or so I thought). In His grace, God provided for my growth and continuing walk with Him. This has included the fellowship, encouragement, and challenge of other men and women through the Officers' Christian Fellowship, Navy chaplains, and many excellent churches. God has been absolutely faithful to me and my family over the years, regardless of whether I have been or not. He has loved, led, answered, convicted, forgiven, and amazed me time and time again. I am so grateful to Him for bringing me to Him so many years ago.

In 1967, I married Margie, and we have been blessed with three children and eight grandchildren. After graduation from the Naval Academy in 1962, I served on active duty as a submarine officer until I retired as a Captain in late 1991 after almost thirty years of active duty. I served on five submarines and had shore and staff assignments. I was in command for almost nine years; my commands included a nuclear attack submarine, a major nuclear training command, and a squadron of attack submarines.

To understand the context of my testimony, here are some characteristics unique to my service in submarines. A nuclear submarine has a crew of about 150 men, living and working inside a forty foot-diameter steel tube several hundred feet long, propelled by a nuclear power plant, "flying" like an airplane, hundreds of feet underwater, self-sufficient, traveling in all the world's oceans, conducting important and sometimes dangerous missions.

Positive aspects of submarine service:

- Working with exceptionally competent people and developing life-long bonds of friendship through experiencing arduous challenges together
- Growing personally and professionally in a well-regarded occupation with high, challenging standards
- Job satisfaction from being granted important responsibilities
- Positively influencing others, contributing to their lives and professional growth
- Learning about and operating interesting and cutting-edge technology
- "In the arena" with the satisfaction of doing noble but hard, risky work of great worth for the country

Negative aspects:

- At sea a lot. In the 14 years I was assigned to specific submarines, we were underway at sea for about half the time. This makes raising a family difficult and is particularly hard on wives and children.
- Highly stressful occupation owing to the technical complexity, the need for attention to detail, and accountability
- Isolation from the fellowship and encouragement of loved ones and other Christians
- Lack of privacy. (My only private space was my bunk with a curtain I could draw.)
- All-consuming life and difficulty of pursuing other interests (e.g., "smelling the roses")
- May foster an independent, prideful, "I can do it all" mentality

I believe that all of the above characterizes the spiritual battlefield that my loving and all-powerful Heavenly Father ordained for me. The positive and negative aspects of submarine service were in constant tension, particularly the aspects related to my family, requiring me to seek Him to sort them all out. My favorite Bible verse, which is inscribed on our wedding bands, is Matthew 6:33: "But seek ye first the kingdom of God and His righteousness, and all these things will be added to you." Starting very early in my career, Margie and I frequently reviewed my decision to remain in the Navy but ultimately felt that God wanted us to continue serving. In all of the decision-making, we prayed, searched the Bible, and sought the counsel of others.

God was absolutely faithful ("great is Thy faithfulness"), even though I frequently was not. Some examples:

- I was forced to seek Him; I came to the end of myself plenty of times and was forced to cry out, and He was ALWAYS there.

- God provided opportunities to influence others for Him through attempting to live out Matthew 6:33, being good at my work, taking care of my men, supporting my boss, and taking initiative. I volunteered to be the Protestant Lay Leader on board, leading Sunday devotions and augmenting the ship's library with Christian literature.

- Ashore, God provided spiritual encouragement through Officers' Christian Fellowship Bible studies and some wonderful churches and chapels. Margie and I either participated in or led an OCF study at every duty station. The OCF was exceptionally helpful in taking care of Margie and the family when I was at sea.

- God provided me with encouragement and challenge through the influence of other men.

- God was/is the father to me in the Parable of the Prodigal Son because I am both the younger and the older brother. Like that father, God gives me unconditional love and acceptance. He also ensures that, like the younger brother, I am miserable in my sin and then grants me the gift of repentance.

- God provided career opportunities consistent with the abilities and responsibilities He gave me. There were jobs I aspired to that would not have been a good fit, and He orchestrated the "right ones." In several cases, He sent us to duty stations other than the ones we asked for, but I praise Him for each of these because the results proved to have been the best for us.

- God blessed me in answered prayer in all sorts of ways including restoring relationships; wisdom in disciplinary matters such as at Captain's mast; dealing with difficult bosses and subordinates; wrestling with moral issues; dealing with broken equipment; living with unreasonable requirements; facing hard tactical decisions; answering "arrow prayers" when there was only time for me to react instinctively and/or I was tired, confused, etc.; protection from my dumb decisions; and safety and peace for me and my family when we were apart.

After leaving the Navy twenty-four years ago, I worked in the commercial nuclear power industry, held several other jobs, have been active in the Officers' Christian Fellowship, have held many leadership positions in our local church and other ministries, and currently serve as a Blue & Gold Officer for the Naval Academy. This season of my life has included the transition from military to civilian life, becoming an empty nester, three weddings, the joy of eight grandchildren, and retiring again. It has also had its challenges because of the inevitable aging process, both physical and psychological, the loss of identity and sense of purpose I enjoyed in the Navy, and seeking and waiting for what God wants me to do now.

My testimony is written in hindsight at age 74 (with much scar tissue), but with a recently-renewed appreciation for the fragility of life, which was reinforced by the deaths of family members and friends and by my own near-death experience.

Several things God is convincing me of today:

- I want to cherish and deepen my relationship with my Heavenly Father. This means nurturing it, abiding in Him through His Word, praying to Him with thanksgiving and repentance, and fellowshipping with other believers. A senior Christian officer told me when I was a midshipman to "bring the Pilot aboard" every day.

- I want to nurture deeper relationships with my family, friends, and the people God has allowed to be in my sphere of influence. I see this as meaning really engaging with people, being an active listener, and striving to love and understand them as God does.

- I do not want to waste this gift of life and relationships with Him and others by continuing to sin. Sin is a distraction and dilutes and impedes these gifts. I know it is part of my nature, but it is stupid. He has provided grace and power, and I disrespect Him by not resting in what He has given.

I may not always trace the onward course my ship
    must take,
But looking backward, I behold afar its shining wake,
Illumined with God's light of love, and so onward I go,
In perfect trust that He who holds the helm the course
    must know.

                                —Anonymous

Captain Greenman can be contacted at rpgreenman1@bellsouth.net.

THE MAKING
OF A CHRISTIAN

Herb Sprague, USNA Class of '62

I often wonder, if I say to someone, "I am a Christian," what image does that bring to mind? I suspect that many (or perhaps even most) might think that I simply grew up in a Christian home or culture, and that I generally agree with most of the Christian principles. I may or may not attend church routinely but generally identify myself with the Christian religion. For lack of a better name, I would call this a "cultural Christian." On the other hand, if you were from other parts of the world, say from a Muslim nation, you would probably think that I was just another American, a participant in all the violence and loose morals they see in American news and films. To them, "Christian" is just another label for Americans, their decadent culture, and all that comes with it. Now suppose, however, that instead of saying that I am a Christian, I say, "I am a follower of Jesus." What image does that convey?

The truth is, I was born a "cultural Christian." I grew up in a Christian home and a Christian culture. I simply grew up knowing who Jesus was, or perhaps who everyone else thought He was. Christianity was something we did on Sundays. But that was a long way from making me a "follower of Jesus."

It wasn't until I was in the middle of my high school years that I started to get personally involved with who Jesus was. I began to realize that Jesus was not just another biblical prophet or a great preacher who taught everyone to love each other, turn the other cheek, etc. I began to read the Bible myself and listen carefully to others, paying particular attention to what Jesus actually said and did. I found that Jesus made some very radical statements about Himself. For example:

- "I am the way, the truth and the life. No man comes to the Father but by Me."
- "I and the Father are One."
- "If you have seen Me, you have seen the Father."
- "Before Abraham was, I AM!"

It seemed that Jesus was clearly saying that He was actually a part of the almighty God Himself. No ordinary man says these things. Also, no ordinary man restores sight with a touch, raises people from the dead, or, for that matter, comes back to life himself after being executed. I concluded that either Jesus really is who He said He is, or He was a very elaborate hoax. There isn't much middle ground. I also observed that those who knew Jesus best, those who walked and ministered with Him every day, subsequently gave up their lives to tell others who Jesus is. They certainly did not believe He was a hoax.

I guess this is basically the question that hangs in front of all mankind. Is this Jesus actually God's Son, a real part of the living God? Furthermore, if He is indeed God, the God who created the universe, and who created me, then perhaps I should really listen to what He has to say, and even do what He says. I came to the same position as the Roman centurion who watched as Jesus was crucified and said, "Surely this must be the Son of God!" Believing this, my next step was to do as He offers, to commit my life to be His follower, wanting to do what He says, and live my life in fellowship with Him. Thus I became a "follower of Jesus." That is what *I* mean when I say, "I am a Christian."

I would like to say that life became easy and glorious after that. However, I found that life had a lot more "up its sleeve," and that my Christian life was just beginning. The next big event—I graduated from high school! Almost instantly, I left all the comfortable places, family, and friends, that I had grown up with. Before I could catch my breath, I was on a plane to Washington, D.C., then on a bus to the Naval Academy.

Talk about a shock! Everything was different, hard, unforgiving. One of the first things that happens at the beginning of Plebe Summer is the arbitrary assignment to bunking with other roommates. My new roommates* were nothing like the guys I grew up with. I had never before heard such "strong" language (to put it mildly)—a vocabulary that, up to then, I thought was reserved for the toughest guys on the football team. As Dorothy would say, I wasn't in Kansas anymore. Amidst all the shouting, running, and chaos of those first weeks of Plebe Summer, I felt really alone, like I had never been alone before.

What was I doing here? How was this young, naïve kid going to survive this new world? How would my Christian faith and life fare in the rough and irreverent life at Annapolis?

As it turned out, or as God had planned it, my Plebe Summer Company Officer was a new '58 graduate, Ensign Otto Helweg. He was a big, tough guy who had been the previous year's Brigade Boxing Champion. During the first couple weeks of Plebe Summer, while we were out learning to march, Ensign Helweg went through all the rooms of his Plebes. I first learned of this when I received a summons to appear in his office. I expected to face some kind of discipline. Ensign Helweg asked me to stand "at ease," then explained that in his tour of the rooms, he had noticed that several Plebes had Bibles among their possessions. He asked if I, along with the other Bible-owning Plebes, would like to periodically meet in his office for a Bible study during our off time. I'm sure you can imagine what wonderful relief this was. I discovered God's world included the Naval Academy,

---

* One of my Plebe Summer roommates, the one with the "really strong" language, contacted me at our 40th class reunion. He wanted to tell me that his life had changed, that he had become a Christian, and he was now an Episcopal priest. Praise God!

too! Those Bible studies anchored my faith, connected me to new friends and fellowship, and gave me the courage to drive head-on into my new military life. I thank and praise God for Ensign Helweg.

As Plebe Summer ended, we braced for the new academic year and the ominous "return of the brigade." And of course, when they did return, we realized that Plebe Summer was just a pleasant "summer camp" compared to life with the brigade. We were all reassigned to new roommates. I had two great roommates, John LaVoo and Tom Draude.

In the course of all the upper-class "running" of the Plebes, a couple second-classmen from across the hall started to befriend us. We weren't "spooned," but they took a soft posture in offering us help and advice. On one occasion, one of them mentioned that he had observed we had Bibles in our rooms and that he'd seen us going off to extra-curricular Bible studies and Chapel services. He said, "When I came to this place, I was also religious. But then I got over it!" He added, "So will you!"

This struck me like a thunderbolt. Was he right? Was this new academy life going to wipe out who I was? In retrospect, I think that shock was really good for me. My two roommates and I all took it as a challenge. We each individually decided this would not happen to us! We would not let the world or the Naval Academy defeat our faith in and relationship with God. To make a long story short, we all graduated from the USNA with a stronger faith, more firmly rooted in God's truth and righteousness. Our time at the Academy strengthened rather than weakened us. It was a time of great spiritual growth.

I would like to acknowledge the many faithful Christians in my academy life who built themselves into me and into my growth as a Christian. I was quickly linked into the fellowship of the OCF (Officers' Christian Fellowship), then called the Officers' Christian Union. We were blessed with the leadership and spiritual guidance of the local OCF representative, Jim Wilson, a Naval Academy grad who also ran the Bible bookstore on Maryland Avenue. He is a mentor with whom we have had continued contact and relationship to this day. It was also his influence that led a young (cute) Annapolis high school girl into a relationship with Jesus; some four years later, she became my wife. Another person who encouraged me was Chaplain Greenwood. While many chaplains were often more involved with their "office," Chaplain Greenwood got involved with us. But the most significant blessing and encouragement to my academy life and my Christian life was my own classmates, those dear guys who also believed in Jesus and who were committed to following Him in their careers and lives. Now, over 50 years later, they remain my dearest friends. I am forever grateful.

Let me conclude with one final thought. Some people may think that Christians are either very noble or very foolish to turn over their lives to a religious concept. They think of religion as sacrifice, being bound to a moral code, giving up "self-destiny," and missing the fun of life. However, these are among the most profound of Satan's lies. God offers us a way of life that reflects His very character and that He knows leads to real life, freedom, and happiness. He guides us away from the snares of sin and all the pain and regret that they bring. For me, faith in Christ has meant freedom, liberty, and joy. It is standing in the very presence of God and feeling the warmth of His goodness. It is looking forward to an eternity that will never be separated from His light and truth. I thank the Lord for who He is and that He cares enough to lead a lowly Plebe into a rich and full life and into His eternal family and presence.

Herb Sprague can be contacted at hos42mls@yahoo.com.

A NEW DIMENSION
TO BEING FAITHFUL

Col. Lee R. Bendell USMC (Retired),
USNA Class of '50

A s a Marine officer, I have sometimes asked groups I am speaking to, "Do you know the Marine motto?"

"Once a Marine, always a Marine," was one confident response. But generally someone comes up with the correct answer: *Semper Fidelis*, "Always Faithful." This motto has been most significant in my life.

I enlisted in the Marine Corps during the closing months of World War II. A year later, I received an appointment to the U.S. Naval Academy, graduating with a commission as a Marine Second Lieutenant—just in time to go to Korea after my Basic Officer Training.

During an engagement with the enemy, I received a round through my elbow, an injury severe enough to call for treatment in a U.S. hospital. While I was still an outpatient at Bethesda, I married the beautiful girl, Gloria, whom I had met while training at Quantico. (We had become engaged before I left for Korea.)

Following various assignments, and now promoted to Lt. Colonel, I found myself back at my alma mater, the Naval Academy. Among my meaningful responsibilities was working as officer representative with the midshipmen by administering their honor code.

When we become responsible for transmitting value systems to other people, it is very natural to take a good look at ourselves: am I really qualified to be the source of such guidance? What is there about my character that gives me the qualification to impart values and standards of ethical conduct to others?

We had moved into a neighborhood where several of the neighbors exhibited qualities in their family life that Gloria and I admired. Many of these neighbors were on the civilian faculty of the Naval Academy. As we became friends, they invited us to join Bible studies held in their homes.

About the same time, I came into contact with a previous classmate of mine who was running a Christian bookstore in the town of Annapolis. During one of our visits, he posed the question, "Lee, are you a Christian?" I recall hemming and hawing a bit, and then saying, "Well, uh—uh, I guess so," thinking only of my regular attendance at church. But his question stayed on my mind.

Then we were invited to a group called the Officers' Christian Union (OCU). The combination of these various Christian influences was causing me to reappraise my life and its purposes. My attempts to be "always faithful" had been limited mostly to those areas that involved the performance of my military duties. I began to perceive new applications of these words to my personal life.

SEARCHING THROUGH REASON

I kept hearing that faith was something personal that had to be exercised not in my speech, but in my heart. I had to have faith that Jesus Christ was the Son of God, that He died for my sins, and that He was resurrected. A believer in Christ should know in his heart that these events took place the way they are described in the Bible. Did I really believe this was so? Here was a test of my personal faith.

I had been indoctrinated with the concept that problems exist to be solved. So I set out to see if I could believe—could exercise the faith that the Bible indicated was a prerequisite to salvation. My scientific education had taught me to collect all pertinent facts, to organize or categorize them, and from these facts to draw certain conclusions. This reasoning process would then allow me to make decisions about the course of action I should follow, soundly based on the factual evidence I had collected.

Most of my research about Jesus necessarily had to be in the Bible. Yet I didn't seem to find the quantity of data that would form an acceptable basis for sound conclusions of reasoning. I couldn't prove to my own satisfaction that Jesus was the Son of God. I couldn't prove to my satisfaction that He rose on the third day. I couldn't believe—couldn't exercise faith—based on the reasoning process that I had been taught.

CAN A CAREER MARINE BE A CHRISTIAN?

I think we all approach momentous decisions with anxiety about what we are going to be forced to give up. I was a career Marine. How would the exercise of real faith affect my military career? Could I even stay in the military and be a Christian? Perhaps the commandment "Thou shall not kill" was bothering me somewhat. A combination of helpful items seemed to answer my questions. An article by Lt. Gen. Harrison in an OCU magazine addressed one of the issues squarely. It helped explain that the real meaning of the commandment was "Thou shall not *murder*," that time and again God had used military persons and wars to achieve His purposes. Military men, like policemen, might be required to take a life in the performance of their duties, and would not be disobeying that commandment in doing so. As Jesus later taught, what counted was what was in their hearts.

Most encouraging to me personally was the New Testament's description of Jesus' encounter with a Roman officer, a centurion, who had come with a request that Jesus heal his servant. I was impressed with Jesus' reply. He didn't tell this officer to get out of his military occupation. No—instead, Jesus said, "Verily, I say unto you, I have not found so great faith, no not in Israel" (Matt. 8:10b, KJV). Then Jesus told him to continue his regular duties. And his servant was healed in the same hour.

Nevertheless, if I was going to exercise faith, I had to have a solid basis of authority upon which to do it—something that could be consistent wherever I might go.

THE AUTHORITY OF THE BIBLE

I found verses in the Bible that helped me understand more clearly the faith that was required of me. For example, Romans 10:9, John 1:12, 3:16, and 5:24, and Ephesians 2:8-9. Yet I could not really accept these verses until the authority behind them was settled in my mind.

Finally, the Bible itself seemed to answer the question of authority. I recalled the Roman centurion of Matthew 8. He had seen Jesus' word as authority and had believed that His command would be carried out. I didn't have Jesus in the flesh today, but I did have His Word. 2 Timothy 3:15-17 seemed to speak directly to me: "From a child thou hast known the Holy Scriptures, which are able to make thee wise unto salvation through faith which is in Christ Jesus. All Scripture is given by inspiration of God, and is profitable for doctrine, for reproof, for correction, for instruction in righteousness: That the man of God may be perfect, thoroughly furnished unto all good works."

That was what I needed. Here was the authority that the words I read in Scripture were written by men who were inspired by God. If I accepted these words, I would be corrected and instructed and perfected and prepared to do good works for God. When this thought permeated my mind, the verses on faith and salvation came to have new meaning. I could admit that I was a sinner, that I fell short of God's intention for me

(Rom. 3:23). Certainly all I deserved was death, but through faith I could receive a free gift from God: eternal life through Jesus Christ our Lord (Rom. 6:23). I came to the point where I could truly believe in my heart that Jesus was and is God, and I could trust that God had raised Him from the dead. I took that step of faith in February 1965. I finally realized a deeper meaning of being faithful—to be full of faith—faith in Christ Jesus. And with this faith came the sense of a close personal presence of Christ in my life confirming that faith. Time and again, God has proven Himself to me as "always faithful"— through the rigors and dangers of being a battalion commander in Vietnam, through my attempts to be a Christian father and husband, through His leading that I should retire from a still-promising Marine career, and through His guiding Gloria and me into the work as directors of Personal Enrichment Clubs of America with the Narramore Christian Foundation. Here we continually sense the Lord's blessing, and we know that our lives are being fruitful for His glory. His faithfulness strengthens our faithfulness.

Once a Marine, always a Marine? Yes, in the sense that my motto and aim is still *Semper Fidelis*: to be always faithful, not only to country and Corps, but to God and in my service to others.

This is the new dimension of being always faithful in my life today: to be ever full of faith!

Written in 1977. Lee Bendell is now (2016) in the Veterans' Hospital in Fullerton, California, on full disability due to the effects of Agent Orange while serving in Vietnam.

FAITHFUL CHRISTIANS
SHOWING ME THE WAY

Dave Wilson, USNA Class of '62

I was just beginning the second semester of my freshman year at the University of Colorado when I received word from my congressman that I had been selected for a first alternate appointment to the United States Naval Academy, and I needed to be sure I maintained a B average to be eligible. I buckled down, and in due time I was informed that my principal had been appointed to the United States Air Force Academy, and I had been selected by my congressman to attend the Naval Academy. I was ecstatic, as was my father, who had served in the Royal Navy in both World Wars.

My parents were both from Scotland. It was customary there to send the children off to boarding school. Since I was the youngest of five, I was sent to Sunny Hills Lower School from fourth through sixth grades and then Sanford Preparatory School on the same campus from seventh through twelfth grades. My future wife, Katrina Konstance Čakste, joined our class in eighth grade. When we first met, we did not become instant friends, as she didn't speak English, and I was so quiet that she wasn't sure if I did, either. But in due time, we became good friends, although we were never sweethearts in high school.

Katrina was born in Riga, Latvia, a year before I was born. Her grandfather, Jānis Čakste, was the first President of Latvia from 1922 until he died in 1927. Her father, Konstantīn Čakste, had left a professorship at the University in Riga and entered into politics, taking over the leadership of the underground government. He was taken prisoner by the German Gestapo, tortured in Riga, and sent to Stutthof concentration camp in Poland. He eventually died in a death march toward Gdansk as the Russian army was proceeding westward with their undisciplined troops, ravaging both the land and the population.

Katrina, who was six years old, escaped Riga with her mother, Anastasia, and sister, Anna. They were lifted onto a moving train of boxcars with what few belongings they could carry and traveled to the west coast of Latvia near Ventspils, where they hid in a barn from some German soldiers. As they walked through the woods on a very dark night, Katrina was almost left behind when she fell into a hole in the ground with her backpack and became hopelessly wedged in place. Fortunately, her mother, who was following behind, managed to pull her out. When they reached the beach after sliding down a large sandbank, she was placed in a rowboat and taken to a fishing vessel. She was passed from hand to hand up a cargo net, and when the last man grabbed her, he ran across the deck and dropped her into a fishing net in the cargo hold. But poor Katrina thought that they were throwing her over the side into the Baltic Sea because she was too much trouble, and she let out a bloodcurdling scream and called to God. It was then that she saw the face of Jesus. When she found herself in the cargo net, she was very disappointed, as she would have preferred to be in the arms of Jesus.

After living in Sweden for six years, Anastasia managed to invest in a sailboat along with a few other families, and they sailed across the Atlantic Ocean under perilous conditions. They arrived in Boston Harbor after surviving a hurricane and a dense fog. Anastasia, Anna, and Katrina were classified as refugees and sent to Ellis Island where they stayed for three or four months until President Truman signed a bill allowing them to enter the United States. I knew nothing of this adventure for many years, as it was too difficult for my wife to share.

Katrina and I shared mutual responsibilities serving on the student court and student council during our senior year at Sanford. Upon graduation, I wrote in her yearbook that before she got married, I wanted to meet the lucky man and give my approval. Little did I know that I would be he.

After one year at the University of Colorado, I entered the Naval Academy as a nominal Christian. I had not attended Sunday school since my second grade year on Belvedere Island near San Francisco, and I had never read the Bible. I was baptized and confirmed in the Episcopal Church, but no one had ever asked me if I knew Jesus. I had one good thing working for me—my mother had been praying for me for ten solid years. Her prayer was simply, "Dear Lord, do something to him."

My roommate for three years was Robert Yohanan, a committed Roman Catholic. With very little fanfare, he rose early almost every morning to attend Mass, and he slipped back into the room about the time the wake-up bell sounded. Suffice it to say he made a huge impression on me.

Well, God is good, and he sent a midshipman to our room to ask Robert if he would be willing to be the thirteenth company representative to the Naval Academy Christian Association. Robert declined with a smile and said, "I am a mackerel snapper, and I belong to the Newman Club." For some reason I piped up and said that I would like to take on the role. The representative gave me a quizzical look as if to say, "You?" but he wrote down my name nonetheless. Looking back now, I realized the Hound of Heaven was pursuing me even then.

When our first class year rolled around, I was apprised of the first Sunday night gathering of the Christian Association. Don Shinnick, the star linebacker for the Baltimore Colts, was to be the speaker. When I arrived, another middy greeted me, saying, "I have not met you before. My name is A. J. Egerton."

I replied, "My name is Dave Wilson."

Then A. J. said, "When did you come to know the Lord?"

I didn't know what to say. So he invited me to come by his room the next day at 1730 hours. I tried to put him off for a couple of weeks, but he persisted. I went to his room, and he shared his version of the four spiritual laws developed by Campus Crusade for Christ.

That is when my search began. I attended a few midshipman-led Bible studies and a prayer meeting in the Chaplain's office at 0530. I visited the Christian bookstore in Annapolis owned and operated by Jim Wilson, a graduate of the Naval Academy. He gave me a couple books to read and led me in a prayer to accept Jesus into my life. After hearing him speak a few times, I came to consider him my spiritual advisor.

After Christmas vacation, I made an appointment with Chaplain Greenwood and asked him if I could lead a Bible study in my company. He smiled. "You can read, can't you?" He gave me some suggestions of where to begin and how to be a group leader. So I went to each platoon and announced that there would be a Bible study in the wardroom at 2100. Much to my surprise, seventeen midshipmen came and shared their knowledge of Scripture, which made my role as the group leader quite easy.

It was about the same time, just after the Christmas vacation, that Katrina came down from Boston for a weekend, and we committed to enter into a Christian marriage. We had been engaged for a year, but we had never talked about the spiritual dimension of a marriage relationship. One direct question from a classmate had led to my conversion, and it was then that I discovered that Katrina already had a relationship with Jesus. Once we talked and made a commitment to a Christian marriage, a wonderful peace came over both of us.

I took another important step in my spiritual pilgrimage by memorizing packets of Scripture verses prepared by an organization called the Navigators. One verse that carried great meaning for me was Revelation 3:20. Jesus says to the Laodiceans, "Behold, I stand at the door and knock: if any man hear my voice, and open the door, I will come in to him, and will sup with him, and he with me" (KJV). This verse spoke volumes to me. I discovered that Jesus wanted me to invite Him into my life, and He wasn't going to force Himself on me.

There is a famous painting by Holman Hunt in St. Paul's Cathedral in London depicting this verse. Jesus is standing by the door that is shut, and there is no handle on the outside of the door. Jesus will only come into our lives when we invite Him in. However, when we do invite Him into our lives, we can be confident that He will never disappoint us.

Katrina and I were married at the Naval Academy Chapel the day after graduation, with Chaplain Greenwood officiating, with a perfect reception at the Officers' Club afterwards. Katrina's sister was the matron of honor, and her sister's husband, an Army captain, walked her down the aisle. My brother was my best man, my sister was a bridesmaid, and eight of my best friends were sword bearers. Admiral Stump, a friend of my father from WWII, gave an impressive toast. We began our honeymoon in the Pocono Mountains of Pennsylvania, then drove slowly westward, ending up in Colorado for a nice long visit with my family, as I did not have to report for flight training in Pensacola until the end of July.

While living in Pensacola, we attended a Presbyterian Church every Sunday for about seven months. That was our first step in figuring out what it meant to have a Christian marriage. When we moved to Milton, Florida, for the next phase of my training, we decided to attend a small Episcopal Church, the denomination my parents had belonged to their entire lives. The rector and the people received us warmly. Katrina was confirmed there, and our first daughter, Kristina Yvonne Wilson, was baptized there.

After receiving my wings of gold, I was given orders to a helicopter training squadron based out of Imperial Beach, California, just south of San Diego. As so often happens in the Navy, we hurried to get there only to be told to wait for a month before I could begin the training. So I volunteered to assist the chaplain in his ministry.

During that month, I had my first wake-up call regarding the danger of flying in the military. In order to get flight pay for that first month, I had to fly as a passenger for four hours, so I called the operations office to arrange for some flight time. I was told I could go up that afternoon or the next morning. I chose the morning flight. Had I gone in the afternoon, I would not have returned. That helicopter went down over the Pacific Ocean, and everyone on board was killed.

That near-death experience got me thinking. Since Katrina had lost her father when she was six, I began to rethink my commitment to being a pilot. I was reluctant to talk to anyone about my fears. I did speak with a flight surgeon, but I was not able to express what was bothering me. I remained shut down for a time, especially with Katrina and my peers. I distinctly remember sitting by myself in a classroom deep in prayer beseeching God for guidance. All of a sudden, I heard

His still, small voice assuring me that He would protect me and keep me safe. Once I left that classroom, I never experienced that kind of fear again.

One of the instructors in the Replacement Air Squadron invited Katrina and me to attend a Bible study in his home. I was still very immature in the faith, and as we drove to his home each week, I would pray that I would not be asked to open or close in prayer. I was terrified of praying out loud. Eventually I was asked to pray. I blurted out something that I'm not sure was coherent, but it got me over the hump, and soon I became comfortable praying out loud. So worship, Bible study, and prayer became part of our daily and weekly routine as we slowly matured in the faith.

After four months in the training squadron, I joined my seagoing squadron and started my first seven-month cruise on board the aircraft carrier *U.S.S. Yorktown* two days before my twenty-fifth birthday in October 1964. We heard about an impending war in Vietnam, and we thought we might be ordered to leave two months early, but that was a short-lived rumor. Katrina flew to Hawaii during the two weeks our ship was in port, and I was able to take ten days' leave, allowing us to enjoy a second honeymoon.

Once we reached Japan and made a port call, the *Yorktown* and a number of support ships were given orders to report to a location in the Pacific where a Russian submarine had been sighted. Our ships spent sixty-four days at sea tracking that submarine until it surfaced. One of our officers spoke Russian, and as soon as the sub surfaced he communicated with the crew on the same frequency we were using. We quickly discovered that the Russian crew was learning as much about us as we were about them.

When we finished tracking that submarine, we set sail for Sasebo, Japan, for a port call of about ten days. That was when the United States declared war against North Vietnam. The *Yorktown* was ordered to report to the Tonkin Gulf where we remained for fifty-four days.

During this phase of the cruise, my crew rescued a downed pilot. But we were unable to rescue another crewman who couldn't free himself from his parachute, and we watched him drown. It was very upsetting. He was a chief petty officer who had not been properly trained in parachute procedures, and I am sure there was a reprimand that followed for the officer who made the decision to allow him on that mission. When we returned to the *Yorktown*, the squadron flight surgeon tried to calm our nerves and offered us some brandy, which helped.

In addition, we lost one of our helicopters on a night mission along with its crew of three men: the pilot, the co-pilot, and a crewman. It was presumed that the generator had malfunctioned, and all the instruments had failed when the batteries ran out of power. The crewman was due to return home the very next day for a new assignment. Once again, I was faced with a need to grieve; but I did not experience the fear I had when I first arrived in California.

During that first cruise when we spent so much time at sea, I think I read every Christian book in the ship's library. In addition, I began to develop a more mature prayer life. I was a slow learner in terms of my spiritual formation, but determination had become my strong suit. I kept a daily journal on that cruise which I still have, and it is a good reminder of the baby steps in my pilgrimage.

When we returned home, I was one of the pilots given the privilege of flying off the ship the day before it docked in the Long Beach Naval Yard. Katrina and Kristina met me at Ream Field in Imperial Beach in matching outfits. Kristina was two years old, and she was talking up a storm. It was a wonderful reunion. While I was away for those months, Katrina and Kristina had a nice prayer time before bedtime each night, and Katrina always pointed to a picture of me when they prayed for my safety. When I came home, Kristina would not let me out of her sight. Some of the other children her age were a bit afraid of their fathers for a short time, so I was blessed.

Soon the squadron was preparing for another seven-month cruise, one totally given to search and rescue. We were assigned to five-week attachments aboard attack carriers, and most of the time we were stationed in the Gulf of Tonkin. Katrina planned to meet me in Sasebo after our first stint on station. As we passed Okinawa on the way there, I was flying plane guard for several pilots who had flown out for carrier qualifications. One of them was having a hard time hitting the center line of the *Yorktown*'s flight deck. The last time around he landed way too far left, and his plane went off the port side of the ship and hung by its tail hook. The pilot and co-pilot climbed out with their life vests, and we rescued them. They were very embarrassed and at the same time very thankful.

Katrina made it to Japan around time the *Yorktown* sailed into the port of Sasebo. It was very risky for us to arrange this rendezvous, as nothing was a sure thing during the war. We were able to spend the better part of two weeks together in the officers' quarters, the very building the Japanese used to plan the attack on Pearl Harbor. Katrina was six months pregnant with our second child. We learned that Japanese women did not go out in public when they were pregnant, so quite a few people stared at us when we were touring.

I was a member of the Officers' Christian Union, which publishes a list of current Bible studies all around the world. We met a Navy dentist and his wife who led a study in their house, and they befriended us in a wonderful way. They invited us into their home for a delicious meal and became our tour guides, showing us some sights we would have never seen without them.

Our time in Japan was a bit tense, as we both knew I was to be deployed on the attack carriers for five weeks, so the fellowship was most helpful. Katrina and I began each day together with prayer and reading the Bible, which brought us into the peace which passes all human understanding. It was hard saying good-bye because we knew our baby would probably arrive before I returned home from overseas.

After the *Yorktown* departed Sasebo, the members of my detachment made preparations to transfer three helicopters and all their support equipment and personnel to the nuclear-powered carrier *Enterprise* anchored in Subic Bay in the Philippines. When we were back in the Tonkin Gulf, each team flew every other day while on station. Some of our missions were thirteen hours long with refueling from destroyers. We would hover over the fantail of a destroyer, lower our rescue hoist, bring the refueling hose up, insert it into the fuel valve, and the ship's crew would send up the needed fuel.

Every other day I attended a noon service in the Chapel. One day I volunteered to lead a meditation. When I finished, a second-class petty officer came up and said I should become a preacher. This caught me by surprise, as I was just beginning to feel that God was calling me into full-time ministry. I spent a lot of time in prayer, usually concluding that God couldn't make a pastor out of an engineer type who had become a pilot.

The last day on Yankee Station, I was on a mission to drop confidential documents onto a destroyer near the south of North Vietnam, then take a navy ensign to another ship to the north. As we were leaving the destroyer and heading north, we received a "May Day" call from an A-6 bomber pilot; his plane had been hit by a missile, and he and his bombardier navigator were bailing out. We were the closest chopper. The area was about one mile off the coast of a city called Vinh and about a mile from the Island of Hon Matt, both heavily armed.

We rescued the injured pilot in short order. While we were doing that, an A-4 attack plane was hit, and its pilot had to bail out. We flew to the other side of the island, rescued that pilot, then returned to search for the bombardier navigator, but to no avail. We took one hit through the tail pylon but made it back to the *Ranger* safely. For these rescues, the entire crew received the Distinguished Flying Cross.

When I returned to the *Yorktown*, I learned that Katrina had been in the hospital in danger of giving birth to our baby much too early. She was very anemic, so much so that the doctors even tested to see if she was suffering from leukemia. My mother had flown out to San Diego to help with Kristina, but that was not her strong suit. After communicating with the Red Cross, I was given emergency leave and returned home about a month before my ship. Katrina gave birth to Anastasia Mona Wilson on August 1st, my father's sixty-sixth birthday. It was a very blessed day for our family.

We remained in the San Diego area nine more months before my final assignment in the Navy as an instructor at a training squadron in Key West, Florida. Those nine months in California meant that we had ample time for family bonding and church participation. We belonged to St. Mary's by the Sea, and we became very involved. While I was away on the second cruise, the priest we had grown to love so much was called to a much bigger church, and the bishop assigned an African-American priest who befriended us. He invited me to join an Old Testament Bible study course taught by a monk on the other side of San Diego. We drove there together every Friday night, and even though it was probably the most boring class I have ever attended, the drive was worth the excursion, as the fellowship was so good.

The year in Key West was our best year in the Navy. I was always home at night, and we could have all our meals together. We joined St. Paul's Episcopal Church and volunteered to teach the fifth- and sixth-grade Sunday school. We were told there were no funds for a curriculum, so we decided to spend the year teaching about the adventures of St. Paul. We made fancy maps of the Mediterranean Sea and the surrounding countries and traced all of Paul's journeys as we read the stories from Acts and related them to Paul's Epistles. By the end of that year, we all felt we had a personal relationship with St. Paul, as he had influenced our lives so much. The children in the class were so eager that they would come to church on their bicycles if their parents couldn't make it.

I truly loved serving my country in the Navy, but I knew I wasn't to be a career Naval officer. I was not happy to see our country become so involved in the Vietnam War for such a long time, and I was very disillusioned to see how the politicians made so many of the decisions about how the war was to be conducted. I lost a number of classmates in that war; many more became prisoners of war and were treated in an inhumane way. After my assignment in Key West was up, I put in my resignation and returned to my home state of Colorado with my family.

Throughout my life since I left the Navy, I have continued to thank God for directing my path to Sanford Preparatory School where I met Katrina and then on to the United States Naval Academy where I accepted Jesus as my personal Lord and Savior. Praise God for his faithfulness!

Dave Wilson can be contacted at father_dave@comcast.net.

HOW I BECAME
A CHRISTIAN

Otto Helweg, USNA Class of '58

was raised in a rural community (a city of 2,000), Watervliet, Michigan, and was in one building from kindergarten through the 12th grade. There were about 53 in my graduating class. I was a "big frog in a small pond" and did everything from sports (football and basketball) to music (band and glee club). I was voted the outstanding boy in the graduating class and prided myself on being moral. (My unspoken creed: "I don't drink, smoke, or chew nor go out with the girls who do.") I was president of the Methodist Youth Fellowship and had pins for perfect attendance in church for something like 12 years. At church camp, I learned my first dirty joke, but after that was active in the Boy Scouts.

We had the stereotypical science teacher who was, at best, an agnostic, but a very good teacher. I liked math and science and wondered if there really was a God, but not being much of a deep thinker and enjoying my reputation as a "shining light," I had no desire to rebel or question the theology of the day. That is, I thought God was a celestial score keeper; when I did good things, I would get a good check, and when I did bad things, a bad check. In other words, I (like so many churchgoers) thought I had to earn my way into heaven. If, when I died (and I never thought of this), I had more good checks than bad checks, I would get into heaven.

The problem, of course, is that if God "grades on the curve," you can never be sure if you will receive a passing grade. Who knows how many good and bad checks you have? But we don't think about those things much. I disliked "religious people," the kind that carried big, black Bibles or demonstrated any kind of emotion.

I had three scholarships upon graduating from high school: one to the University of Michigan, one to the Coast Guard Academy, and one to the U. S. Naval Academy at Annapolis. I chose the latter. I am not sure how it happened, but I started attending a pre-reveille prayer meeting my Plebe (freshman) year. I suppose I figured I would get double credit from God for such a sacrifice. I also sang in the chapel choir and played sports (football, boxing, and lacrosse).

During the Plebe year at the Naval Academy, life is tough. You only get two leave periods your first year, one over Christmas and the other for spring leave. An upperclassman asked me if I would like to go to a Christian conference over spring leave. I could think of about 500 things I would rather do than spend this valuable leave period in what I figured was a weekend of church. I politely declined and went to New York with a friend where we went sightseeing and attended some concerts.

However, by the time I was a second classman (junior to you non-military types), spring leave was no big deal, so I accepted the repeat invitation to this conference. It was inexpensive, and I could take my girlfriend along, so it would not be a total loss. This conference was sponsored by the Officers' Christian Fellowship for Naval Academy midshipmen and West Point cadets.

Upon arriving, I could see this was a big mistake. First, I felt completely out of place, sort of like a person walking into a high mass in cutoffs and "go aheads."* Second, I thought I was surrounded by a bunch of hypocrites. Everyone was smiling and pretending (I thought) to have a good time. As time went on, I realized they really *were* having a good time.

The big surprise was that my stereotype of a religious person was shattered. Previously, I considered religious people to be weak physically and mentally, social outcasts who had to flee to church groups to find acceptance (e.g., a tall skinny kid with glasses). It never dawned on me that my theology was inconsistent. Here were midshipmen whom I highly respected. There were cadets against whom I had played sports. There were officers who were outstanding, especially a marine major who was head and shoulders above any of

---

* Flip-flops, referred to as "go aheads" in the 1950s because they would fall off your feet if you tried to walk backwards

the company officers at the Academy, both in physical ability and mental sharpness.

Also, the speakers were great. They were Dr. Robert Smith, a philosophy professor from Bethel College, and Rev. Keefe, a Presbyterian minister who was a baseball "nut" and spoke on (of all things) Habakkuk and Haggai, Old Testament books I hadn't heard since I had memorized their names in Sunday School for some kind of prize.

God, with His sense of humor, chose a "tall skinny kid with glasses" to corner me at the conference and ask if I was a Christian. The "skinny kid" was Jim Wilson, a graduate of Annapolis, and was now on the staff of the Officers' Christian Fellowship. Since I defined a Christian as someone who was going to heaven and I didn't know the status of my good checks and bad checks in God's score book, I couldn't answer his question.

I told him that I went to church and asked if he didn't think I was a Christian. He said that if I didn't know, how could he know? He asked if there was a time in my life that I had accepted Christ into my life. I answered that I didn't know. Did you have to do something like that? He said that there was no set formula, but normally a person becomes a Christian by making a specific decision.

By that time, without analyzing why, I was feeling very uncomfortable. I now know that his question suggested that I was *not* a Christian and that my whole theological foundation might be wrong. This implied that all of the good points I thought I had accumulated by attending boring church services and pre-reveille prayer meetings might not exist. I

didn't want to consider this and rather abruptly excused myself. Jim's parting words were to go to the source, the Bible,
which any good scientist would do, to find out God's defini-
tion of a Christian.

I returned to the Academy and conveniently forgot about
the conversation at the conference. Several weeks later, I received an invitation from Major Perrich, the Marine company officer I had met at the conference, for a Sunday lunch at
his quarters. I could also bring my date.

In my pseudo-modesty, I assumed that Major Perrich had
recognized my superior leadership and was inviting me over
to further my career. However, when I arrived, who should
be there but Jim Wilson, the guy that had cornered me at the
conference. I may not be too bright, but I could see that this
was a setup. Major Perrich had invited me over so Jim could
corner me again.

Sure enough, after lunch, they managed to get my date to
help with dishes so Jim and I wound up in the living room
alone. He asked me if I had thought any more about our conversation. I answered, "A little," which was the overstatement
of the year. He then asked if I would like to pray with him and
make a decision to give my life to Christ. I answered that I
didn't think I was ready to do that.

At that point, for the first time in my life, I was presented
with the way a person can become a Christian. Jim explained
that when we are born physically, we are dead spiritually, in
a natural state of rebellion against God. The rebellion may be
very subtle, like being religious while keeping God comfort-
ably at a distance, running our own life, living for self.

Jim continued to explain that there were two ways to get into heaven and find spiritual life. One was to be perfect (which even I could see was beyond my capabilities; it was already too late) and the other was to accept a gift from God. That is, imperfection (sin) cannot exist with God. It is like a harmful bacterium trying to live with an infinitely powerful antiseptic; it would be obliterated once it came within a million light years of it. In order to approach God (and heaven), we need to be sin-free.

This is a dilemma. God is just and cannot merely wink at our rebellion, but God also loves us. How He solved this problem is the greatest story ever told. He entered our time-space continuum in the form of a man, Jesus, and lived the perfect life for us. He then paid the price for our rebellion by allowing Himself to be crucified. He proved that this sacrifice was acceptable by rising from the dead, and He offers this as a free gift to be received by faith.

Faith, in the Bible, is not merely mental assent, but actually trusting on Christ alone for forgiveness and adoption into God's family (eternal life—heaven). All I needed to do was accept this gift and give control of my life to God.

After hearing this, I knew in my heart that it was true. There was a self-authentication in the message. Consequently, when Jim asked again if I would like to accept this gift and give God control of my life, I said, "Yes!" As I knelt down to pray, I wondered what this would cost. Most military people understand commitment, and I wanted to be sure I could accept the demands of this. I thought of the "worst-case scenario," which, at that time, was that God might send me to be a missionary in the deepest part of Africa. That thought was so abhorrent to me that I put it on the shelf of my mind, agreeing to go ahead whatever the cost, even if I was not sure I could pay it.

After my prayer to give my life to Christ, I was rather disappointed, because there was no surge of emotion—no flashing lights, etc. However, I had made a commitment. Major Perrich and his wife congratulated me. I was a little embarrassed in front of my date but left wondering what was in store. Major Perrich counseled me that now I belonged to God, Satan would send doubts into my mind and I should reject them. I thought this sounded like kidding myself that something was real when it was not. Nevertheless, I determined to spend several minutes in prayer every evening before bedtime and read a chapter out of the New Testament.

You need to remember that, externally, I was a very moral person. The fact that I was really a hypocrite (Pharisee of Pharisees) had not entered my mind. As I look back, it is an act of grace that God's Spirit opened my heart because (I'm embarrassed to say) I had no sense of sin. Everything was going well: studies, sports, personal relationships. I am convinced that the reason I understood the truth of the message Jim brought was because someone had given my name to a group of Christian officers whose wives made it a point to pray for midshipmen.

This decision happened decades ago, and while God never promises a problem-free life for His children, He does promise to be with them and give them the means to overcome all problems. I can attest to that. Having Christ at the center of your life just makes sense. Why would anyone want to make ill-informed decisions when he or she could tap into the wisdom of their Designer and Creator who knows the beginning from the end? Assuming you are not a mechanic, which makes more sense when your car has problems: lifting the hood and aimlessly turning screws, wiggling wires, etc. or having the engineer who designed it take over?

In spite of having a wonderful wife, a great job, and three super sons, I cannot wait to get into heaven. If God were to give me the choice to die now or wait, I would jump at the chance to be with Him.

CHRISTIAN LEADERSHIP TRAINING IN THIRTY NATIONS

Mylan "Myles" Lorenzen, USNA Class of '62

n June 1958, a young Nebraska farm kid checked into the Plebe Summer for the Naval Academy class of 1962. It was my first time on a commercial airline, and I joined a soon-to-be-classmate and his dentist dad to fly from Omaha on our way to the Academy in Annapolis, Maryland. I thought I was pretty hot stuff, being the first graduate of Neligh High School in recorded memory to go to one of the military academies. I had spent the first eight years of my education in a one-room schoolhouse with outdoor toilets. And here I was going to Annapolis. Wow!

At the time, I was a nominal Christian. My hard-working farm family of Northern European extraction attended the first

Congregational Church of Neligh whenever the alfalfa hay did not have to be put up or the corn picked. I was moral, at least outwardly, and clean-cut. If someone had asked me, "If you died tonight, would you go to heaven?" I would have answered honestly, "If God won't take me into heaven, who in the world would He take?" In my 17-year-old arrogance, I could little have imagined the breaking process that God had in mind for me.

The Plebe year at the Academy was very tough. But I had enough stubborn German blood running through my veins that I was not about to let them bust me out with all the hazing. I made it through bruised, but unbroken! What followed was an exciting Youngster Summer cruise on a destroyer to escort the young Queen Elizabeth on her Royal Yacht *Britannica* and President Eisenhower on a naval cruiser into the Great Lakes to open the new Saint Lawrence Seaway.

My first watch on the ship was a mid-watch (midnight to 4 AM). It was in the boiler room in the deepest bowels of the ship where the steam that powered the destroyer was generated. Trying to keep cool beneath the 105-degree air blower while struggling to keep my supper down, I miserably concluded, "I don't even know if there is a literal hell; but if there is, this has to be it!" My two-month exposure to the Navy in action left me wanting to go Air Force upon graduation. Brokenness was progressing nicely, thank you!

It was during the following Youngster (or sophomore) year that God really began to work on my heart. The pressure of Plebe year was over. But I was 3,000 miles away from my close-knit family, which had moved from Nebraska to California, and I simply did not know who I was or why I was there. I became acutely aware of a huge void in my life. I was surrounded by the best and the brightest from all over the world. My first exposure to life on a Navy ship had not been all that fulfilling. Not to be deterred, I began to focus on my academic life. Let's pump up the grades! Yet that didn't seem to fill the void.

During this time of deep personal emptiness, I met some classmates who marched to a different drum beat. They reflected the intriguing vision that there was more to life than grades, beer, sex, and career. These guys (no girls back then)—Cal Dunlap, AJ Egerton, John Knubel, Larry Yandell, Tom Uber, John Lavoo, and others—accepted me as I was, with all of my inner turbulence. They befriended me and invited me to a Bible study (of all things).

The study was taught by Jim Wilson, who ran the Officers' Christian Union bookstore on Maryland Avenue just outside the Academy main gate. Jim's bookstore was an evangelistic organization. I became hooked. Although church attendance was mandatory back then and I sang in the chapel choir, I really had little spiritual foundation. I was so intrigued by Jim's opening up the Scriptures and teaching practical truth that applied to young men in our situation. The Bible became alive under his tutelage. It was the Gospel reflected in both the Scriptures and the lives of my new friends that begin to draw me to Jesus. I bought my first Bible, a Cambridge King James Version, from Jim's bookstore and began to read it on my own.*

In the fall of 1960, as the Bible was coming alive in my heart, I came to faith in Christ. I saw that He was God—God

---

* I still have that Bible, well-marked-up and smelling of diesel fumes from my early days in submarines. It is one of my most prized possessions.

the creator, who emptied Himself and became a man in human flesh. I learned that He lived a perfect life—the only human being to have ever done so. I learned that He surrendered himself to a gruesome, grisly death on a cross. It hit me like a ton of bricks that He had done that to die in my place. I learned that because of His love, He gave His all so that He could give me eternal life. Then, miracle of miracles: God raised Jesus from the dead, never to die again, to prove that His sacrifice for us had been effective. Jesus was alive!

Wow! In the words of Jesus in John 3, I was born again. To quote Jim Wilson, it was "like having a bath on the inside." I had a deep sense of forgiveness and joy. His Spirit began filling the void. Peace began to move the inner turbulence aside. I found a sense of vision and purpose for life that transcended a Navy career. I discovered a deep sense of camaraderie and fellowship with my friends who had already experienced this new birth.

Together we began to prayerfully work at sharing this life-changing "best of all possible news" with our classmates and others at the Academy. Life would never be the same. Under Jim's mentoring, many of us began leading evangelistic Bible studies in our company areas in Bancroft Hall. By God's grace, we even got to witness some in these studies experience the same transformation we had been privileged to taste. We were given opportunities to share our testimonies and even occasionally to preach. A vision for ministry began to take shape in my life.

Thanks to Jesus, a "green behind the ears" Youngster midshipman who was ready to resign from the Boat School in disillusionment and turmoil found life and would stay at the Academy and then enroll in the Navy's Nuclear Submarine Program to serve Him there. A year after graduation, in 1963, I was privileged to marry the love of my life, Carol Jeanne Schmidt. Fifty-three years later, as I write these words, Jesus' LIFE has never failed to fulfill and bring change. Today, totally by God's grace, we are blessed with three grown and married children and nine grandchildren (ages 14 to 26), all walking in authentic and honest ways with Christ. Jesus continually proves His love and faithfulness, despite two bouts of cancer for Carol and myself; a crippling and as yet undiagnosed neurological disease for our son-in-law, Tim; a congenital and life-threatening disease for our 15-year-old Mattie Jeanne, and a recent Alzheimer's diagnosis for Carol.

Following my discharge from the Navy in 1969 and graduation from seminary in 1974, Carol and I have been privileged to spend forty-two years of vocational ministry doing evangelism, church planting, and leadership training in nearly thirty countries around the world. Through all these marvelous experiences, the Lord's breaking processes have continued. The Gospel—God's total provision for my total need—has become more beautiful and powerful. The cross of Christ has become increasingly central to all aspects of my life. Slowly but surely I'm learning to make it my boast (Galatians 6:14). This verse of a familiar hymn captures where my heart is now:

> I take O Cross, thy shadow,
> For my abiding place;
> I ask no other sunshine,
> Than the Sunshine of Your face.

Content to let the world go by,
To know no gain nor loss,
My sinful self, my only shame,
My glory all the Cross.

At seventy-five and approaching retirement from active ministry involvement in World Team, I'm dedicating the remainder of my life to learn how to more faithfully walk in the Spirit in pursuit of this three-fold purpose:

- Enjoy Jesus always!
- Encourage Carol and others in the Gospel,
- Using presence, words, and drawings!

Myles Lorenzen can be contacted at mylanlor@comcast.net.

MY INTRODUCTION TO
AND WALK WITH CHRIST

Doug Powell, USNA Class of '62

I was born in Miami, Florida, on April 28, 1940. My father had migrated to Florida from a farm in Georgia, and my mother from a farm in Indiana. We did not regularly attend church, but somewhat ironically the two times a year we did attend, Easter and Christmas, it was to one of my father's sisters' churches, a very emotional Pentecostal church.

Sometime in my late pre-teens, I started attending a Southern Baptist church a few blocks from my house. I didn't come to know Christ at that time, but I did learn a lot about the Bible. Actually, I was only going to a Sunday school class, but once a month that teacher would take us to the church service afterwards. I remember him always wanting me to go forward when they did the invitation at the end of the service, but I don't recall him ever explaining what going forward meant. In any case, there was no way I was going to go down there in front of all those people. I attended for quite some time, but I don't remember exactly when I stopped going.

In junior high, I worked one class period a day in the school library. I really got attached to a girl who worked there with me. One day she asked me if I would like to go with her to a youth meeting called the Christian Youth Ranch. The "Ranch" was held in the home of a couple, Ray and Sue Stanford, who held meetings for different teenage groups on different nights of the week. When we arrived, we would play games for a while, then go inside and sit around and sing some hymns. Then Ray would bring the message, almost always focused on Ephesians 2:8-9: "For it is by grace you have been saved through faith—and this is not from yourselves; it is the gift of God—not by works, so that no one can boast." I attended for several weeks until the man who picked a few of us up altered his route so that I was the last one to be dropped off. I remember sitting and listening to him in the car in front of my house. I don't recall what he said, but I am sure he was sharing the gospel with me. It was too personal, and I soon stopped going to the Ranch.

Three or four years later, in my senior year of high school, one of my teammates on the varsity basketball team invited me to go to a meeting. I didn't realize until I got there that it was the Ranch! But I was more secure by then and didn't feel threatened. I was again exposed to the gospel. At a beach party for the kids at the Ranch, I realized that at some point I had put my faith in Christ, and I knew that I was saved. It was also at the Ranch that I met Jean, my wife-to-be.

That was in November of 1957. Shortly afterwards, I received my appointment to the Naval Academy. During Plebe Summer, we were in our room one afternoon when the Officer of the Day came to the door. We jumped to attention, and he asked whether Mr. Powell was there. I replied, "Yes, sir!" and he ordered me out into the hallway. I was terrified, wondering what horrible rule I had violated that would make the O.D. personally come to my room.

But the O.D.'s name was Otto Helweg. He said that someone from my hometown had called the chaplain's office and told them about a young believer in the Plebe class. He told me about a Bible study that was being held weekly down the hall. I started attending. During the study, I learned about the Officers' Christian Union (now Fellowship) and this guy ministering outside the main gate in a Christian bookstore. I ventured out one Saturday afternoon and had my first meeting with Jim Wilson.

Over the next four years, Jim had a great influence on my life. No one else has ever come near shaping my spiritual growth as Jim did as a Christian mentor both in word and by example. During my four years at the Academy, I either attended or led Bible studies, visited Jim at the Christian bookstore in town, and was involved in numerous other Christian activities. Upon graduating in 1962, I opted for a commission in the Air Force instead of the Navy in order to have more time with my new wife. I stayed in the Air Force for eight years, the first two and a half as a Titan II ICBM crew deputy commander and the last five and a half flying, mostly as an instructor pilot in the supersonic T-38 Talon. At the various bases on which I was stationed, I either attended an existing Bible study or started one in our home. During that time, I was privileged to fellowship with a number of very special Christian brothers and sisters.

I left the Air Force in 1970 and relocated to Dallas, Texas, where I have lived ever since. My family attended a couple of different Bible churches before joining the group that started the Fellowship Bible Church, pastored by Dr. Gene Getz. The original strategy of FBC was not to build a mega-church, but to start numerous churches around the Dallas metropolis and ultimately around the country. I served in a leadership role there and helped to form several spin-off churches over the years. I led a Bible class and occasionally preached. It was there that I met Myles Lorenzen, one of my classmates from the Academy who had come to Texas to attend the Dallas Theological Seminary. Our families became close, he and Carol having two children roughly the same age as ours.

I have two children, both followers of Christ, and seven grandchildren. After thirty-two years of marriage, my wife decided to leave and eventually filed for divorce. It had a mild impact on my walk with the Lord, but in His grace, a year later, He brought Marcella into my life. We were both staying at a bed and breakfast in Branson, Missouri, she to visit her son who was working with Campus Crusade for the summer. We had only a little time together, but something clicked, and I wrote her a letter when I got back to Dallas (she lived in Chattanooga). This began a long-distance relationship until we were married in 1994. God used her to deepen my walk with Him and to expand my ministry.

God has blessed me far more than I could ever deserve. That's called grace. My walk with Him is 24 hours a day, trying to remember to thank Him for every detail He blesses, minute by minute. My goal is to be in contact with Him constantly, no matter what I am involved in, which means everything from major issues to solving crossword puzzles.

Doug Powell can be contacted at dpowell@niwcorp.com.

BLESSED BEYOND BELIEF

Cal Dunlap, USNA Class of '62

LIFE BEFORE A PERSONAL RELATIONSHIP WITH CHRIST

I grew up in a loving family that was made upwardly mobile by my father serving as a Navy radioman in World War II, my mother insisting that my father complete his GED and go to college after the war, and our nation graciously enabling him to attend the University of Tennessee, then grad school at Cornell University on the GI Bill.

My mother saw to it that I went to church. My German immigrant grandfather's evangelical church made sure I attended a summer church camp where I first heard the claims of Christ, although I didn't understand the truth of those claims.

In high school in Beaver, Pennsylvania, I was a member of the United Presbyterian youth group. At church summer camp I made an intellectual commitment to who Jesus was and what He had done for me. It was a struggle to tell others about it. There was only one person in my high school class who was really public about her faith. Yet my minister hoped I might go to seminary. I would have called myself a Christian if asked, but I was not sure that others would have seen how my life differed from theirs. As a leader in high school, I remember my English teacher bringing me up short for my pride.

A seventh-grade teacher at my school told wonderful stories of her son who had attended the Naval Academy. My appointment to the Academy was a dream come true. Great sea stories, my father's naval service, and the wonderful USNA scholarship gave the hope of a military profession that prized and developed character-based leaders. Yet I still had little sense of a personal spiritual life.

HEARING GOD...HOW

Towards the end of Plebe year in 1959, I met a group of midshipmen that lived differently than others. Then everything changed.

A classmate had invited me to attend a meeting of the Officers' Christian Union in St. Andrews Chapel. My heart was warmed by the exposition of the Scripture in dynamic and convicting ways. As the OCU representative, Jim Wilson, spoke with great power, I felt the need to know Jesus personally and not just intellectually. He was to be Lord of my life, experienced daily. It meant a new direction. Now I know that I was "hearing" God.

The next big surprise was the validation of the gospel message in the lives of my Christian classmates. I wanted to be like them. You could live as a Christian in the Navy! I thrived in the fellowship with, and the encouragement of, these classmates. Years later I would read of the Cambridge Seven, a Royal Military Academy cadet and six Cambridge students who in 1885 dedicated themselves to following God to China. This "band of brothers" was like what happened in the USNA Class of '62. God's touch on each one validated His presence and the truth of the gospel message in the lives of the others. You believe something because you believe that it is true, not because of what it does for you. Over fifty-five years later, I still believe the gospel to be true. But even intellect itself can fail. In those times, memories of His great faithfulness validate my belief.

How I Responded to This Radical Change

One of the first changes was that I began to love my roommates and the guys in my company, especially the Christians. Through Jim Wilson's ministry at the OCU bookstore on Maryland Avenue, I began reading Christian books and at his encouragement took *Through Gates of Splendor* by Elisabeth Elliott on my summer cruise. The cruise included the opening of the St Lawrence Seaway and a visit to Milwaukee for repairs when our destroyer hit a sandbar in the St. Clair River, which connects Lake Erie and Lake Huron.

Jim started me on the Topical Memory System of the Navigators. Because of the repetition involved, I still remember many verses half a century later.

The weekly OCU meetings acquainted me with Scripture. Eventually we also had company Bible studies. Later my classmates would meet for prayer in a small chaplain's office behind the steps to Memorial Hall. I joined several Christian classmates in teaching Sunday school to the kids of the Naval Academy Chapel families.

It seemed imperative for the brigade to hear more of Jesus. What if Billy Graham could visit USNA? I contacted Grady Wilson on the Graham team and asked if Reverend Graham would come to Annapolis. It seemed impossible, but what a faith builder when he spoke at the USNA Chapel at Christmas 1961! That was the first time that Billy spoke at the Academy. What a thrill when the chaplain invited some of us to lunch with Billy at his quarters after the service.

As a midshipman, my vision for the world expanded rapidly through hearing national evangelical Christian leaders speak at the USNA. Bill Bright, Doug Coe, Frank Laubach, Corrie Ten Boom, and Cleo Buxton encouraged us to follow Jesus closely. Cleo, the executive director of the OCU, persuaded a group of classmates and me to attend the Inter-Varsity Christian Fellowship Urbana Missions Conference during Christmas break my last year at the Academy. The conference was held at the University of Illinois; about 9,000 college students were encouraged to see their lives as part of God's plan, not just for their country, but for a needy world.

MAJOR WORKS OF GRACE IN MY LIFE

During midshipman years, I had a special relationship with a high-school sweetheart. But with my new spiritual commitment and the distance between our two colleges, we drifted apart. The person you marry is the second most important decision you make in life. It takes a special spouse to handle the pressures and temptations that come to a military family, especially during deployments and separations. God sovereignly protected me in the choice of a wife. It took many years to realize that His plan was always better, even though pain might be involved in the process. I did not know at the time that the greatest joys and pains during the next fifty years would center around the godly women that God brought into my life. I lost two fantastic wives to cancer and married a third time. Each loss brought great pain. But with each loss, I continued to grow stronger in faith and trust in a good God and Savior who interceded for and strengthened me. David's painful example (I Samuel 30:6b ESV) where his wives were taken from him was very helpful to me: "But David strengthened himself in the Lord his God." God did the strengthening, but it was also my decision to trust Him. I found great mystery in this faith process, but learned not to let the things that I didn't understand interfere with the things that I did understand.

Another act of Jesus was my calling to a life work. While graduation from the Naval Academy seemed to indicate that a naval career was ahead, a few years after graduation, the questions loomed. Was God leading me to stay in the Navy and accept the offer of postgraduate education at the Naval Postgraduate School and Stanford University? Or leave the service and accept the offer from InterVarsity Christian Fellowship to become a staff worker at a university campus? God's direction became clear at Campus by the Sea, IVCF's summer camp, where I was on leave as a counselor to college students. I was called to the military and to marrying Elizabeth.

Earlier, I had picked up a small card in an IVCF-related bookstore in Hong Kong during a port visit. On the card was a Chinese scene and a verse of Scripture: "Those with Him are called and chosen and faithful" (Revelation 17:14b ESV). While I did not see Jesus with my eyes, I felt sure of my call, and that brought great comfort in my marriage and career and the adversities of life. After my beloved Elizabeth's death fifteen years later, I married Linda, my vivacious second wife. After my retirement from the Navy and from being a civilian research professor at NPS, we served six years together as the OCF staff members at the USNA, the very position that Jim Wilson had twenty years earlier. Upon Linda's death another twenty years later, my devotional life suffered. After almost thirty years of joint devotions, I was on my own. As I prayed or read Scripture, my mind would wander. God was so good to bring lovely Michelle into my life at age 73 to resume a joint devotional life that has been such a treasure.

Among the wonderful blessings that God has provided are our children: Chris J, Jon D, Carl J, and Chris D. Blending families is very difficult, even when both sides of the previous families are godly! One of the main reasons for marriage is to raise children and grandchildren that reflect God's glory. All the pain of merging families is worth it in the end, as the godly reflections are evident later in their lives.

But how do you keep growing in faith? In my twenty years of active duty, I found that a weekly inductive Bible study in a professional peer's home was key to growth in the Lord. The OCU/OCF Bible studies provided applications from Scripture for both family and professional life. At each duty station I sought out a study or started one. On shore assignments (Monterey, California, and Oahu, Hawaii), we saw great growth in the number of these studies and in the numbers of folk who came to know Jesus personally.

About ten years after retiring from the Navy, I was asked to be the executive director of the Association for Christian Conferences, Teaching, and Service (ACCTS). ACCTS is a sister organization to OCF founded by Cleo Buxton in 1972 to take the gospel to military folk in all nations of the world.

Just as this new job started in 1994, Linda and I learned one of the greatest spiritual lessons of our lives—the daily dynamic of living in God's grace. For the first thirty years of my spiritual life, grace was only a salvation word such as in Ephesians 2:8-9. But Paul's calling to minister a chapter later was also based on God's grace. "Of this gospel I was made a minister according to the gift of God's grace, which was given me by the working of His power. To me, though I am the very least of all the saints, this grace was given, to preach to Gentiles the unsearchable riches of Christ" (Ephesians 3:7-8 ESV). This major work of God's grace was to change my leadership and marriage. I began offering grace to others and not assuming that I deserved anything because of my position, qualifications, or rights. Each day of health, time with family, and my leadership position were undeserved gifts of God.

My twenty years on the ACCTS staff allowed me to work with Christian military leaders from over a hundred countries. Military retirement afforded me enough money to work with ACCTS on a very modest salary for many years. God faithfully took care of our sons' education and provided for potentially crippling health bills through retirement health benefits.

Why write about these things? Because I am thankful for God's blessings and desire to celebrate His goodness and reflect His glory. Therefore I hope that some will awaken to their spiritual calling from Jesus: "Behold, I stand at the door and knock. If anyone hears my voice and opens the door, I will come to him and eat with him and he with me" (Revelation 3:20 ESV). I hope that Christian midshipmen or cadets will be encouraged to intentionally develop strong friendships with other Christian classmates and find that these significant relationships can last a lifetime of bringing glory to God. They have four years to do this, or this treasured opportunity may be lost.

I hope that officers will seek out or start a regular weekly Bible study such as the ones offered by OCF or other Christian ministries to help with the process of Christian growth throughout their careers. Lastly, I hope that those about to retire will consider that God has given them the resources needed to shift from a focus on success to a focus on significance, to spread the gospel around the world, perhaps even to militaries in other countries.

Cal Dunlap can be contacted at caldunlap62@yahoo.com.

SIMPLE FAITH,
MARVELOUS GOD,
EXTRAORDINARY LIFE

Tom Uber, USNA Class of '62

This is my journey of faith with insights from my close friend John Knubel, a 1962 classmate at the Naval Academy.

I was born into a strong, Bible-centered family on July 17, 1939. My parents introduced me to the Lord Jesus Christ at a young age. As I always had a strong desire to please Him, I sought the Lord often.

In March 1956 my life changed dramatically—forever! I was attending a youth rally at my church. Reverend Stanly Kendall invited us to ask Christ into our hearts. I can still see him leaving the pulpit and coming down the aisle toward me where I sat at the back of the church. He was on the way

to invite me to come with him to the altar. In such situations
in the past, his attention had angered me. I wanted to be left
alone. My relationship with God was my business; but this
time I answered Christ's call.

I went to the Naval Academy with a strong Christian background tagged with equally strong legalistic leanings. However, my college days were spiritually rich because of Jim Wilson,
who discipled me in the ways of Christ. He helped me understand what it means to be a disciple of Jesus. He encouraged
me in Bible study, Scripture memory, and the steps of faith,
mostly by his example. Jim aided me greatly in wrestling with
the religious legalism I had carried from my youth. Jesus was
setting me free to serve Him out of love, rather than rules and
consequences. This realization started me on a journey of inte-
grating my Christian faith into my everyday life.

For twenty years in the Navy, I experienced the benefits
of small group Bible studies and accountability relationships.
My wife Shirley and I supported Navy life as a family. We also
saw Navy life as a mission field where we could encourage,
strengthen, and share with others Jesus Christ, His Word,
and His way of life. Personal relationships, small groups,
chapel, and the Officers' Christian Fellowship played a large
part in this. Our desire was always to please God and to obey
Him as we continued growing in His likeness.

Upon my retirement from the Navy, I followed that same
pattern in the local church, enabling me to continue growth
in discipleship to this day.

Sometime in the 1990's, two events greatly enhanced my
walk in obedience to Christ. The first was a church seminar

where an invitation was given: "All those who wish to become prayer warriors for God, come forward." I hurried out of my seat. Those steps began new growth in my prayer life! Once more I was experiencing newness in Christ! This has been a continuing journey through the years as I have seen my prayers for others being answered.

The second event involved a course written by Henry Blackaby called *Experiencing God*. Through it I learned that a disciple works *with* God, not *for* Him. I also learned that what the Lord Jesus desires and expects from His followers is a continuing, deepening love relationship with Him.

I am now in my seventies. I rejoice that God has enabled me to follow Him all the days of my life. My life in Christ has become a thrilling adventure in faith. He is by far my best friend, and obeying Him is my passion. I want to be a 24/7 disciple right to the gates of Heaven.

My challenge to you is to come follow Him with me!

ADDENDUM BY JOHN KNUBEL

I've been a friend of Tom Uber's since we met in the fall of 1958 on a football field at the Naval Academy. He has allowed me to write my perspective on his Christian testimony because his attempts to do so have never "quite flowed," probably because he's never been given to focusing on himself.

When I was a boy, my parents described the Naval Academy idealistically (and somewhat unrealistically) as a place where hard work and proven capability, rather than position and privilege, qualified a person. Tom came from a large family whose success is described by "fear of the Lord is the beginning of all wisdom." Neither of Tom's parents had extensive formal education, but they raised their family with Christ at the center and with education as a paramount value.

Tom became a Christian at an early age and came to the Naval Academy with a strong Christian background, but one where grace was subordinate to works. Jim Wilson's primary impact on Tom's Christian journey was to introduce him to the reality that good works flow from grace freely given to the believer. Salvation cannot be earned; it is freely given.

One example of Tom's effort to integrate his Christian faith into his everyday life that impressed me was that while a standout wrestler at the Naval Academy, he constantly gave credit to the One who had blessed him, win or lose, motivated by an ever-present desire to "always [be] prepared to make a defense to anyone who asks you for a reason for the hope that is in you" (1 Peter 3:15 ESV).

Following graduation and while he was serving successfully in submarines, Tom and his wife Shirley lived as missionaries to the military. Their impact was widespread as they raised a family which included several foster and adopted children. While teaching at the Naval Academy, Tom served as the Officers' Christian Fellowship representative and enabled the purchase of Maranatha Mansion just outside Gate Three. Following his retirement in 1982, Tom and Shirley spent over twenty years of hard, dedicated work founding and building His Thousand Hills which continues today as a Christian camp and conference center.

Tom and Shirley's lives of demonstrated dedication testify to the faithfulness of God. Many people were positively impacted as they moved through life expecting the "divine appointments" that give them opportunities to share their faith in their everyday walk. I am one of those people, and I thank God for Tom and Shirley's lives of faithfulness to their Savior that continue today.

Tom Uber can be reached at tsubernc@gmail.com.

TRANSFORMED BY CHRIST

John Knubel, USNA Class of '62

T here are many Scriptures that have played a substantial role in my almost seventy-six years of life. But the best overview of my as-yet-incomplete faith transformation is given in Romans 5:1–5:

> Therefore, since we have been made right in God's sight by faith, we have peace with God because of what Jesus Christ our Lord has done for us. Because of our faith, Christ has brought us into this place of undeserved privilege where are we now stand, and we confidently and joyfully look forward to sharing God's glory. We can rejoice, too, when we run into problems and trials, for we know that they help us develop endurance. And endurance develops strength of character, and character strengthens our confident hope of salvation. And this

> hope will not lead to disappointment. For we know how
> dearly God loves us, because he has given us the Holy
> Spirit to fill our hearts with his love. (NLT)

By grace we are saved through faith. Grace secures us the moment we believe. The Holy Spirit given to us when we come to faith is called a down payment to the promised joy in heaven as well the agent of transformation in this life (see John 13-15). The transformation is far from complete when we believe in our hearts and confess with our lips. I am reminded of the epitaph reportedly on the grave of Ruth Graham (Billy Graham's wife): "End of Construction— Thank you for your patience." That is my story as well. Thank you for your patience in plowing through what follows. For friends and family who have been so faithful with advice and counsel, thank you for your continued patience.

I was born into a middle-class family on July 5th 1939, two months before Hitler invaded Poland. My parents met at a dinner party while my mother was living in New York and singing in the choir at the Metropolitan Music Hall. They fell in love after she encouraged him by putting a can of sardines in his mailbox after learning of his passion for them. They were married in 1934 at a resort in the Poconos in Buck Hill, Pennsylvania.

My mother was the daughter of Milton Kistler, an East Stroudsburg Bank Treasurer. My maternal grandmother, Caroline Smith, whom we called Mamie, and my grandfather headed the Methodist and Presbyterian Sunday schools, respectively. Their home had a somewhat liberal but also controlling spiritual atmosphere.

My father was a civil engineer and architect practicing with his father in New York City. He was born in 1896, bred in New York's Upper East Side, and educated at the Hamilton School for Commerce, an all-boys school. He was raised as a non-practicing Catholic; he came to faith later in life and often watched Fulton J. Sheen in his last years. His mother (Mary Woods) was Irish and died when he was ten. His father, John H. Knubel, was an engineer, deer hunter, and outdoorsman whose family came from Germany in the 1880s, probably through Ellis Island.

My father was attending Lehigh University when World War I broke out, and he joined the Navy. He attended Officers' Candidate School at Harvard and afterward commanded a flotilla of three wooden-hulled sub chasers. He deployed to the Mediterranean and operated in the Atlantic off the East Coast and in the Caribbean. He left the Navy in the late 1920s to return to NYC and business with his father.

After the attack on Pearl Harbor in 1941, my dad rejoined the Navy. He was primarily based in Washington serving in a logistics role with the Navy Department of Munitions. He also traveled the world on special missions and spent his last six months in Guam as part of a reconstruction effort. He left the Navy as a Commander in 1948, staying in the Reserve but never formally retiring because he died at age 63.

Parental relationships are the most important of our formative years. I was brought up by caring parents who emphasized education, faith, and discipline. My dad prepared me for the world he anticipated I would be entering, a world that involved war. He nurtured me to understand what manhood meant: being tender, respecting God, caring for the weak and less privileged, and understanding the unique and distinct role of women in society and the family. He demanded that I work early in life in order to understand the value of the dollar, a discipline I disliked at the time but am thankful for now.

My mother wanted me to have a liberal education and felt uncomfortable with me playing football. My father leaned toward engineering and supported my participation in football. Both expected me to enter military service, get good grades, and "serve my fellow man." My high school years were active and pleasurable; I played a musical instrument in a dance band as well as football and JV baseball.

In 1948, my father moved the family from Washington, D.C., to Scotch Plains-Fanwood, New Jersey. I attended public high school and left in the fall of 1957 for Brown University, which I chose because our football coach, Chuck Nelson, a former Marine, had played for them. Coach Nelson taught me that religion wasn't for weaklings as I had come to believe. He taught me that a man could both play football and pray by publicly leading us in prayer before each game.

A turning point in my faith journey came when our high school history teacher, Mr. Chuck Armerding, invited several of us to go to Madison Square Garden to hear Billy Graham. When Mr. Graham asked Christians to stand up and acknowledge their faith, I could not stay seated, as much as I wanted to. By announcing my faith in front of classmates and friends, I fulfilled the second half of the criteria laid out in Scripture for becoming a Christian: "Believe in your heart and confess with your lips" (cf. Rom. 10:9). Publicly confessing my faith to my peers meant all the difference.

* * *

My freshman year at Brown was confusing. I was moving from a family life where basic needs were met and I had achieved success to an adult world of responsibility, uncertainty, and risk. I was taking courses for which I was ill-suited, and during freshman week, I flunked the eye exam for admission to the Naval ROTC program.

This general confusion, caused by a lack of focus and combined with an ankle sprain and other injuries, ended football season for me. Then incompatibility with a college roommate whose girlfriend became pregnant started me towards a new dream and prayer: to seek admission to the Naval Academy the following June. I started a "pray, plan, and act" process to discover, "What's next, God?" I traveled to Washington, D.C., over Christmas break and gained the support of Coach Nelson and Admiral Spanagel, whom my Dad had kept in touch with since his Lehigh days over twenty-five years before.

Three days before the class of '62 convened, I received a telegram inviting me to enter the Naval Academy. By then, I had had second thoughts about leaving Brown, but I followed through, believing my entrance to the Naval Academy was very much a "God thing" and therefore His will for my life.

My father had his first heart attack on a Saturday morning in 1950 and suffered three more before he died in early January of 1959, during my Plebe year at the Naval Academy. His partnership with two younger men had dissolved in the early 1950s after he was taken ill, and he died in New York City during a business meeting.

I remember him as a very patriotic, loving, caring, religious (if un-churched) man who was critical of organized religion. He helped me by combining criticism with encouragement and affirmation, particularly when I was a teenager. He was buried in Arlington a week after he died. I returned to the Academy immediately after the service to take exams. I held my tears back until arriving at the Plebe dinner table that night and was embarrassed when they flowed openly. The upper class was very understanding. I'll never forget our Company Commander Doug Volgeneau coming to look in on me and ask about my welfare right after dinner.

The Naval Academy was right for me. I threw myself into the program and gave up football and music after Plebe year. I took every extra course I could. I eventually stood high in my class and got a math major. (The class of '62 was the first to be able to major.)

Going to the Naval Academy challenged my Christian faith while also greatly nurturing it. How could I be called to serve in the military and be willing to kill and destroy if necessary, even though it was in the line of duty? Could I trust my government? I answered those questions satisfactorily, benefitting from the example of many currently-serving and veteran Christians—people like Jim Wilson, Tom Hemingway, William K. Harrison (an Eisenhower classmate), Cleo Buxton, and others. It was a time of reaching out and exploring how other Christians lived. The Officers' Christian

Fellowship was an invaluable help during that formative period, as were my USNA friends and Chaplains Greenwood and Kelly.

As a result of my father's passing, I supported my mother in her transition into widowhood while at the same time enjoying bringing friends and classmates home to New Jersey for weekends and vacations. These folks exemplified a simple, solid, wholesome, and attractive faith-based lifestyle. I was able to observe many examples of what it meant to be a Christian from classmates like Myles Lorenzen, Herb Sprague, Bob Greenman, Cal Dunlap, Tom Uber, and also A.J. Egerton, who died tragically two years after graduation. They represented the type of people my parents predicted I would meet at the Naval Academy, namely, people with whom I was able to form lifelong relationships.

Because I was high in my USNA class, I became a candidate for the Burke Program, which included a year at sea followed by an academic experience with the goal of getting a PhD. In 1958-59, the Military Academy received five Rhodes Scholarships featuring Heisman Trophy-winner and football All-American Pete Dawkins. Inter-service rivalry intervened in my favor when I was asked if I would be interested in competing for that program. I interviewed in front of a final selection committee headed by Milton Eisenhower, whom I had hosted in my role as "six stripper" when he was head of the USNA board of visitors. I also had the privilege of hosting Billy Graham, who spoke at chapel, and was able to relate to him my teenage experience at Madison Square Garden.

After a few harrowing experiences in the Barents Sea while on the USS Bang (SS 385), I qualified in submarines under the tutelage of Captain Alex (Mal) Sinclair, another positive role model.

I reconnected with Carole Truitt with whom I had my first date at a church dance on her 14th birthday. Because the Rhodes scholarship required recipients to remain unmarried during studies, I left for Oxford engaged but unable to set a date. My Oxford experience was life-changing both because I was living outside the U.S. and because of the stark differences between the academic environments of Oxford and the Naval Academy. At Oxford, we were told we would receive a battery of tests at the end of two or three years which would determine the degree and grade received. At the USNA, evaluations were frequent, threatening, and sometimes life-changing.

During my first year at Oxford, my relationship with Carole was stressed. In April 1964, we mutually decided to break our engagement so that I could enjoy female relationships at Oxford. Many Rhodes recipients married anyway during that time, putting pressure on the scholarship committee to change the outmoded rule in the spring of 1964.

I pursued the study of economics because of its heavy application of mathematics and statistics. My economics tutor Sir John Stout, an Australian, suggested staying a third year and devoting the extra time to the Modern Greats course with the study of moral and political philosophy, epistemology (the study of words and meaning), political science, and a strong emphasis on economics. I supplemented that with studying comparative economics in Luxembourg in the summer of 1965, where I was accompanied by a very pregnant Carole.

The grace that Carole demonstrated during that saga showed me how much she loved me and made it an easy decision to write in June 1964 to ask her to marry me. We were married on August 29, 1964, the same day as David and Elizabeth Beim and Bob and Martha McNeill, two Rhodes classmates. Our daughter Diana was born December 3, 1965. Being married helped my academic success, and I came home from Oxford with the hoped-for "first"-class degree. I returned to sea duty on two submarines (the *Cobbler* and the *Trout*).

In August 1969, Carole and I moved to Washington, D.C., with our three children so I could accept an economics post in the Office of the Secretary of Defense. We sought out fellowship and joined Bible studies. This involvement and willingness to live out my faith publicly provided an anchor that saved me from many pitfalls in Watergate-drenched Washington. It reminded me daily that I had and ethical "keel" or grounding. Carole encouraged me to be a spiritual leader at home. She was a great source of stability, spiritual connectedness and continuity, a role she continues to play today.

After a year, the position on the OSD staff morphed into one on the National Security Council in an office that advised Kissinger and the President. I worked five and a half days a week, ten plus hours a day.

* * *

My commitment to the Navy ended in June 1972 when I was offered a civilian position on the NSC Staff. The prospect of continued high level-policy involvement made the offer difficult to reject. In the early winter of 1973, David Beim, then an investment banker in New York working with international oil companies, told me an energy crisis was coming. I became an oil crisis "expert" on the NSC staff, best defined by the phrase, "in a blind world, the one-eyed man is king."

My Christian commitment led to a memorable moment when in the midst of Watergate and its many firings and resignations, I accepted administrative responsibility for supporting a Bible study headed by the chairman of the Federal Reserve Board, Arthur Burns.

The period from 1970 to 1974 was filled with turmoil and even tragedy as the American government suffered the storms of Watergate, the Vietnam protests, and the energy crisis of 1973–79. One night, Carole greeted me as I came home from work very late with an emotional but honest, "Sometimes I wish you were back at sea, because then I could at least manage the house routine." Her honesty rocked my boat and drove some sense into me. I might have good intentions, but I was flirting with violating "what does it benefit a man if he gains the whole world but loses his own [and his family's] soul?" (cf. Mark 8:36 NLT). I was in jeopardy of becoming a victim of my own egotistic ambition, although originally my professional ambition had been fueled by the theme, "whatever you do, do it heartily, as to the Lord and not to men" (Col. 3:23 NKJV).

In order to create a new future, I accepted a position at the Chase Manhattan Bank and moved back to New Jersey to be near family. After two years there, I was assigned to Athens, Greece, as a Chief of Staff to the head of the newly-established Middle East Banking Group under Bill Flanz. It was a welcome invitation to learn banking, despite war and instability. We called Dennis MacLeer to pastor the American Church in Greece. I shared a helicopter with David Rockefeller piloted by the Crown Prince of Jordan, who was rumored to have more confidence than competence when it came to flying. It was a rich time seeking fellowship and camaraderie with other expatriates, although it was marred by my mother's going to be with the Lord in September 1973 while I was home on leave.

After three and a half years in Greece, we returned to New York. Again the Lord preserved me personally and professionally although the industry and the bank were in turmoil. There were wholesale firings and downsizing of many offices, including the positions of my peers and all the senior executives I had previously reported to in Greece and New York.

Spiritually, I was supported by friends like Skip Nagalvoort and others with whom I met for early-morning Bible studies. With three girls nearing college age, I realized I needed to leave Chase for something more stable. Through the help of John Bishop, a Marine from the class of '65 who also took his faith seriously, I took a position with a small Orlando, Florida, investment and real estate company.

Carole was a wonderful example of faith lived out as we together managed the difficult job of moving three girls in the middle of high school. Two years later, I was approached to interview for a position with USAA. Carole at first balked at the prospect of yet another move, fearing the impact on the girls. I was stressed and, although I hadn't spoken to him for some time, I went to Jim Wilson for guidance and support for my planned move. I received the guidance, but not the support. Our short conversation went something like this:

"Jim, I feel God is calling us to a new business opportunity that would be very good for the family in San Antonio, but Carole doesn't get it."

His response was short, but helpful: "Until Carole is ready to move, God is not calling you to that job. Turn it down."

It was a big step of faith, but I turned down the second interview. Eventually Carole and I both came to understand the move would not devastate our senior in high school as Carole feared. A phone call from Fred and Marilee Laughlin, friends we met in Washington, D.C., in the 1970s, also encouraged Carole and paved the way for our move to San Antonio that summer.

Life is lived looking forward into uncertainty and risk, but understood as we look back and see the wonderful, sustaining grace of God. Carole and I proved the reality that the closer two individuals in marriage get to the Lord—sometimes on their knees—the closer we get to each other and to the resolution of conflicts.

After three years in San Antonio, we welcomed the move back to Washington, D.C., where the same Christian friend whom we met in the 1970s helped us locate the house we would live in for the next twenty-three years. We were glad to be back in the fellowship of D.C.

After a few years in D.C., I was confirmed by the Senate as Assistant Secretary and Chief Financial Officer of the Department of Housing Development. I also taught political science as an adjunct professor at the Naval Academy, substituting for active-duty officers sent to Iraq unexpectedly.

I reaffirmed the truth of Proverbs 3:5-6: "Trust in the Lord with all your heart, and lean not on your own understanding; in all your ways acknowledge Him, and He will direct your paths" (NKJV). Washington is filled with people who want more political power than they can use responsibly, while New York is filled with people wanting more wealth and money than they can spend responsibly.

What follows here is an outline of some key experiences and observations from a life that has been greatly blessed, enriched, and enabled by the Holy Spirit. It was guided by a simple "life mission" written many years ago to "glorify God and enjoy Him forever. To glorify God in every area of life: personal, family, and professional, and in all my relationships." I have tried to seek ways to openly express my faith and reach out to others in witness. I am a great believer in the admonition attributed to St. Francis: "Go forth and preach Christ, and if necessary use words."

Having fathered three strong-willed and observant daughters, I have learned that actions speak louder than words, and values are "caught more than taught." If you are to have a witness at home and in your vocation, the first thing to pursue is personal and professional excellence as laid out in Colossians 3:17:

"And whatever you do or say, do it as a representative of the Lord Jesus, giving thanks through him to God the Father" (NLT).

I have tried to make these values a driving force in my life. If at times it has led to over-achieving and arrogance when the world has rewarded me, as I'm sure it has, I am thankful that on the downside, when my efforts did not succeed, I had the blessing of knowing that, as long as I have done the best I could and have done it "unto God and not unto man with thanksgiving," I have not failed. God is in control, and life only has meaning and purpose as it is related to faith. Carole has been constant in reminding me of this reality, particularly at key times of testing in our lives together.

It is hard to overstate the importance of having Christian mentors, friends, and of course a good wife. Carole has been continuously gifted with the ability to see God's hand at work in our lives, even when I wasn't looking for it.

As I turn 76, I am buoyed by the reality that "even though our outward man is perishing, yet the inward man is being renewed day by day" (2 Cor. 4:16b NKJV) and that "for to me, to live is Christ, and to die is gain" (Phil. 1:21 NKVJ). My prayer is that both Carole and I can live out our last years with the knowledge that we should not fear death because of the promise of "the hope that lies within us" (cf. 1 Peter 3:15). We can pray to have the comfort of the Holy Spirit and a positive outlook as we approach the drawing of our last breath here on earth. And we know that prayer will be answered because of the down payment already given.

Here are few thoughts that I hope are as meaningful to others as they have been for me as my Christian journey continues:

- In godly decision making, the process is as important as the ultimate decision because, as the Scriptures teaches us, man plans, but God determines the outcome.

- We can control our actions and attitudes but not the outcomes. The higher the level of responsibility, the truer this is.

- It is critical to bring our life partners and others in the family into the decision-making process at the outset. Marriage and leadership as a husband is an exercise in servant leadership, not command.

- To help us along our Christian journey, it takes a village of friends who both love you and seek to serve God.

- If you want a friend, be one. Be proactive in building relationships and nurturing them over time, despite regional relocations.

- The Holy Spirit resides in us from the moment we come to faith. His role is to comfort the afflicted and afflict the comfortable.

- God promises to give us what we need, not what we want. As we study the Scriptures and prove their value in our lives, wants and needs draw closer together.

- A family needs a financial plan from the beginning. Learn this early. A good place to start is to give 10% and save 10% off the top and spend from the remaining 80%. Keep a three-months' supply of cash in the bank; if it is spent in an emergency, build it up again. Paying for a solid asset like a house that will hold its value over time is anathema unless you have carefully planned how to pay for it.

- Share your financial plan with your spouse and other family "stakeholders" and revisit it often as circumstances change.

- Build resistance to sexual temptation before you run into it. Run when it surfaces, as Joseph did in the Old Testament. Avoid the temptation of flirting.

- Rely on and memorize God's promise that He will not allow you to enter into a temptation that exceeds His grace. He will provide grace to resist the temptation.

- What you do as a parent and husband speaks much louder than words. In all areas of life, leadership by example is the only effective model. In the home, the husband's role is self-sacrifice. There is not a hint of command.

- When investigated in the line of duty, if falsely accused, recognize that vengeance belongs to the Lord, not to you.

- Covering up sin is self-destructive.

- We are accountable to God and to His judgment, not to man.

- In marriage, we need to leave our parents and cleave to our wife and whatever children God gives us. I have been so blessed by my friend, lover, helpmate, and life partner, Carole. She is a Proverbs 31 woman.

I hope that life is far from over. But at times, I wish for immediate glory and eternity, for the fellowship and peace that remains mysterious and indescribable until we see God face to face in Jesus the Christ.

John Knubel can be contacted at johnknubel@gmail.com.

SAVED FROM BEING "GOOD"

Jim Wilson, USNA Class of '50

Besides the greatness of the camaraderie that comes from the closeness and the danger, there is something else that I have appreciated from my time in the military. That is that "authority" and "obedience" are good words. The recognition of our mortality is also a great asset.

Here is a little background. I was in the 13th and then the 19th companies in the fourth battalion. I rowed crew for most of four years but never got into a varsity boat except for the first boat in Plebe year.

Most of us who are still alive had narrow escapes in Korea, Vietnam, or the Cold War. I had one remarkable event on the *USS Brush* three months after commissioning. The gunnery officer told me to leave my battle station in gunnery plot and come up to the main battery director. We were at GQ on the east coast of Korea, closing range to destroy some railroad cars. I left the chief fire controlman in charge of plot and proceeded to the main battery director. When I got up to the director, he did not know why he had called me there.

While I was there, we hit a mine on the port side. The explosion obliterated gunnery plot and flooded the forward fire room. We lost sixteen men: six in the fire room, five in plot, four overboard, and one died from burns in the hospital. That evening I conducted the funeral when we buried the chief at sea. He had died in place of me.

Then I spent thirty months on the *Brinkley Bass*, including three two-week stints in Wonsan Harbor in 1951, 1952, and 1953, on the first of which we lost a man on the bridge from shrapnel from a near miss by .75mm that was hidden in a cave on Kalma Gak Peninsula.

Now I am 89. I read in the *Wall Street Journal* that the average life span of an American is 77.6 years. That means that I am now ahead of the average by more than 10 years.

In 1956, I resigned my commission in order to represent the Officers' Christian Fellowship at all of the service academies. I did this for five years, then spent an additional six and a half years at the Naval Academy. Consequently, I know men from classes '57 to '72 (and classes since then, but not as well).

Three major events led to the decision to resign my commission:

- My own conversion to Christ during my Youngster year.
- My battle station men dying, with me not having told them the Good News.
- Many officers and men receiving Christ on the ships and stations I was on. I realized I had a responsibility to communicate the Good News in an effective way.

Many of you already know the Father. Some of you do not know for certain where you will go when you die. Some of you are formally and maybe nominally Christian, some of you are anti-religion, some of you will get angry with me for bringing up the subject, and some of you will really want to know what I am writing about.

Whatever your response or lack thereof, here is, hopefully, an adequate explanation of how to go to heaven when you die. It is possible that some of you will not understand. It will sound like foolishness to you.

I will start by sharing my own experience with you. My father was born in 1899. My mother was born in 1900. They were married in 1924. They had six sons born between 1925 and 1943. I was number two. We were a close, poor, moral, non-religious family. Our parents had very strong convictions, which they passed on to us in two different ways: teaching by our mother and requirements by our father. The result in us was a sense of superiority which today would be called "self-righteousness" or "holier than thou." I did not know the terms, but certainly I thought I was better than other kids. I did not use bad language, either profanity or slang. Neither did I smoke (everyone else did), drink, or run around with girls. I did not think I was a "sinner." I had reserved that word for the real bad guys. Because of this "goody-goody" reputation, I got in several fist fights in eighth grade and a final one in eleventh grade. By my senior year in high school, I had become a little more accepting of my classmates.

World War II started for the U.S. in December of my freshman year in high school and ended the August after my graduation in 1945. I had been very eager to enlist, which I did on May 7, 1945. It was the day Germany surrendered. I was not called to active duty until September 1945. Japan had surrendered the month before.

During my last year in high school, my older brother Leonard gave me two books, one of which was titled *Room to Swing a Cat*. One of the two books—I don't remember which—stated that the Navy selected 100 enlisted men from the fleet every year to attend the U.S. Naval Academy. I made up my mind to attend the Naval Academy, and that book told me how to get there.

While I was in boot camp, I saw the notice for the Naval Academy Prep School (NAPS) and immediately applied. After an interview with a board of officers, I was selected for NAPS. In January 1946, I arrived at Camp Peary, Virginia, a former Sea Bee training base. School had been in session since the fall, so the group that arrived with me was behind. In the spring, 1,200 of us took the entrance exam; 330 passed. I barely passed. The Naval Academy accepted all 330 of us with Secretary of the Navy and congressional and presidential appointments. I entered the Naval Academy in June 1946.

At Camp Peary, I was not a happy camper. I was moral in one sense and insubordinate in another sense. I would argue disrespectfully with commissioned officers. I would jump chow lines with a friend. I did not have many friends. I thought that was the reason I was unhappy. My explanation was that I did not have friends because I did not get drunk or "laid." I was not willing to compromise my morals in order to make friends. But that was not the reason for my unhappiness. Satan has two primary characteristics: pride and lying. I had them both. I lied my way through high school. At the same time, I was self-righteous.

Around January 1946, before going to the Naval Academy, I had received a letter addressed to a Jim Wilson Seaman First Class, Radio Technician, Del Monte, California. I was puzzled, since I had never been to California. It quickly became apparent that I did not know the correspondent; there must be another Jim Wilson. I do not remember the content of the letter other than that there were Bible quotations in it. That embarrassed me. I considered myself moral, but not religious. I sent the letter back to the sender with an apology for opening it. A few weeks later, a sailor came into the barracks and asked for Jim Wilson Seaman First Class, Radio Technician. I identified myself. He said that he was also Jim Wilson Seaman First Class, Radio Technician, and that he had just arrived from Del Monte, California. He had some of my mail. Of course we got to know each other.

I had a real problem with the friendship. Until I met Jim, I had compared myself with everyone I had ever met and come out on the best end of the comparison. This included my older brother and my father. I admired and respected them very much for their intelligence and integrity, but I still I thought I was better. I really was self-righteous.

This other Jim Wilson had me beat. He was more moral than I was and lived it with less effort. He had many friends. He seemed to be happy. He was a brain. He was an athlete. He came from a wealthy, sophisticated home. I felt inferior around him and thought that he was putting me down. He wasn't, but I thought he was.

For two summers in high school, I worked all night in the open air at the Omaha, Nebraska, stockyard. I became fascinated with the stars and learned a little about them. So in order to be up on the other Jim Wilson in something, I decided to spend an evening with him in the open naming the stars to him. He did not need to know their names, but my ego needed a boost, so I bragged.

In the middle of my teaching, he interrupted me. It went something like this:

> Other Jim: "Jim, are you going to heaven?" (No one had ever asked me that before.)
> Me: "I don't know. I will wait and find out."
> Other Jim: "What do you think about it?"
> Me: "I think I will go to heaven."
> Other Jim: "Why do you think so?"

I told him how good I was and how bad I wasn't. If I did not make it, heaven was going to be thinly populated. I was not trying to be funny. He had asked a serious question, and I had answered it seriously.

However, he laughed. I thought he was putting me down. I got angry and retorted that if he was so smart, did he know that he was going to heaven?

He replied that he *did* know that he was going to heaven. He said it with such assurance I could not say that he did not know. I asked him how he knew. He told me of his experience with Christ. He also told me that salvation was not the product of being good or not being bad. It was a gift. He told me that people who thought they would go to heaven because of their good works would not get there because of their boasting. I had been boasting.

In the ensuing discussion, I am sure Jim told me the good news of the deity of Jesus, His death for sinners, and His resurrection from the grave. I did not understand much of what he said. What I thought I understood, I rejected. I think I had fourteen reasons for doing this, but I can only remember two.

First, I did not think I was a sinner. I had reserved that word for the really bad guys.

Second, if salvation was a gift, then the bad guys could get in just as quickly as a nice guy like me. That did not seem right to me.

Having voiced my rejection, I was still intrigued by Jim's life. I asked him where he got all his information. He told me it was in the New Testament. I found one, a pocket-sized King James Version, and began to read it diligently. It made no sense to me. I kept reading it.

The war was over; Jim got out of the Navy and entered Columbia University, while I entered the Naval Academy. Freshman year was like boot camp plus a full academic schedule. I did not try to break rules, but I did talk back to upperclassmen. The result was that I accumulated many demerits. I forget how many was the limit before a compulsory resignation from the Academy, but I was close to it.

In January of my Plebe year, a classmate, Caryll Whipple, saw me with my New Testament. He invited me to a Bible study. I thought it might be a means of understanding what I was reading. I told him I would attend. Then he told me it met at 0545 in the morning. Suddenly I did not want to attend. That was 30 minutes before reveille. When I gave excuses of not waking up, he told me he would wake me up.

The group met seven days a week in a janitor's broom closet. In this group, I met more men like the other Jim Wilson. One of them was Willard (Pete) Peterson, '49. He had been a Christian for about a year. I went to the group for the next three and a half years. Sometimes I would argue, and sometimes I would try to fake being a Christian. In the meantime, my moral willpower was running out. I was a goody-goody to my classmates, but this pre-reveille group knew that I was not a Christian.

The year was finally over. I was in the first boat in the Plebe crew, so while the rest of the brigade of midshipmen went to Northern Europe on summer cruise, I remained for the national crew races at the Poughkeepsie Regatta.

When I finally caught up with the summer cruise fleet, it was in Portsmouth, England. I was assigned to the *USS Wisconsin*, an Iowa-class battleship. One of my classmates fixed me up with a blind date. The two girls were from Northern Ireland. They worked in the Hotel Russell laundry, Russell Square, London. Apparently my classmate's plan (I just followed along.

True, but dumb.) was to buy a bottle of wine and feed it to the girls while necking on a park bench in the square. I did not drink, but I did help purchase the bottle. The girls got drunk. They did not get friendly drunk; they got nasty. I went back to the ship thanking God I hadn't lost my virginity with them.

There was a daily Bible study at sea. It was on the 011 level (eleven decks above the main deck). I was gradually learning, from the Bible and from experience, that I was a sinner.

Back at the Academy my Youngster year, I was again attending the daily pre-reveille study and was still not a Christian. In early October, I turned twenty years old. It was football season. The Navy had a very small stadium, so home games with bigtime opponents were held in Baltimore. Two of my classmates fixed me and themselves up with a triple blind date that we were to meet on the 30-yard line after the game. (Navy only won two games during my four years there. This was not one of them.)

During the game, I realized I would be in trouble, morally, if I went on this blind date. I really do not remember whether I showed up and canceled or just did not show up. In any case, I found myself alone in Baltimore on a Saturday night. The section of Baltimore I was in was not very Christian in its entertainment. It may have been The Block.

I remembered that the Christians who had come to the game had something planned that they were going to, but I had no idea where or what, so I bought a newspaper and looked at church advertisements. There were many. One of them said Saturday night, corner of North Avenue and St. Paul. I got in a cab and went there. There were two churches on opposite corners. The Baptist church was locked, and the Presbyterian church was open. It looked like a few hundred people were there. It was a Youth for Christ meeting. I went up the balcony steps to look over the crowd. There were three midshipmen about five rows from the front. I went down the aisle to sit next to them. One of them was Pete Peterson; the other two were Jim Inskeep and John Bajus, all class of '49. Pete was surprised to see me. The director of the meeting saw us four midshipmen sitting up front and thought we must be Christians. He came down and asked if we would like to testify of our faith in Christ. I replied that I had nothing to say. The other three agreed and went to the platform.

I listened to them tell their personal stories. I had a hard time believing them. I wanted to think that they were lying, that they were hypocrites, but I knew better. They lived the way they talked. It was possible that they were mistaken. If so, they were happy mistaken men. As I said earlier, I was not happy. I envied happy people. There was another alternative: that what they were saying was true and right.

The singing that followed the testimonies was impressive. Then the main speaker for the evening was introduced. He was Filipino. His name was Gregorio Tingson. His text was the first few verses of Psalm 40:

> I waited patiently for the LORD;
> > he turned to me and heard my cry.
> He lifted me out of the slimy pit,
> > out of the mud and mire;
> He set my feet on a rock
> > and gave me a firm place to stand.

> He put a new song in my mouth,
>> a hymn of praise to our God.
> Many will see and fear
>> and put their trust in the LORD. (Psalm 40:1-3)

I remember verse 2 very well: "He lifted me out of the slimy pit, out of the mud and the mire; He set my feet on a rock and gave me a firm place to stand."

After the meeting, Pete took me into another room and introduced me to a saving relationship with God the Father through His Son Jesus. I was ready. I knew that I was a sinner and could not save myself. I called upon the Lord. That was October 18, 1947. Immediately I had joy and peace that I do not recall ever having had before.

I went back to the Academy that night with a desire to tell everyone the good news of Jesus Christ. But then I realized that the Navy would think I was crazy and discharge me. I changed the plan to just telling my roommate and the classmates in my company. Then I realized that they already thought I was too religious (daily pre-reveille Bible study) and goody-goody (no profanity, no drinking). If I told them that I had just been saved from my sins, that would really confuse them. "What sins, Wilson? We've been trying to get you to sin all year!" I decided not to tell anyone.

In the meantime, there were real changes in me that I could see but did not think others could see.

- I had joy and peace.
- The Bible that I had not been able to understand suddenly made sense.
- I found I belonged with the pre-reveille fanatics.

- My conscience was clear.
- My conscience was more sensitive.
- I realized I really cared for my roommate (loved him in a godly way).

Three weeks had gone by when my roommate, Dick Daykin, demanded to know what had happened to me. I asked why he had asked. He told me that I had been unbearably pleasant for the last three weeks. About forty years later, I stayed with Dick in his home in St. Louis. We went out for a prime rib dinner. He asked me to tell his wife what I had told him our Youngster year at the Naval Academy when we were twenty years old. The testimony you have just read is what I told him those many years ago.

Here is a short synopsis of the 69 years since my entrance into the Kingdom. By the time I became a first classman, I was a relatively mature Christian and, with several other classmates, led an underground Christian movement.

Since it was peacetime, I asked for a ship in the Western Pacific with the idea of being an encouragement to missionaries when we were in port.

During my thirty-day graduation leave in a little town in central Nebraska, 25-30 high school and college kids came to Christ. Three of them were my brothers. One adult received Christ; he was my father.

I went on to San Francisco to await transportation to the *USS Brush* (DD745), supposedly in the Philippines. While I was in San Francisco, the North Koreans crossed the 38th Parallel. When the handful of my classmates finally got transportation, it was close to the middle of July. It seemed everyone wanted to go to Westpac. We landed in Okinawa on July 15, where we heard a rumor that Task Force 77 was in Buckner Bay. It was true. I came aboard the *Brush* that day. The Task Force got underway on the 16th. We supported the landing of the 1st Cavalry Division in Pohang on the 18th and rode out a typhoon on the 19th.

After six weeks in a bent-line screen with the carriers *Valley Forge* and *HMS Triumph*, the *Brush* was sent to the front lines of the Pusan Perimeter in Pohang Dong. We spent twenty days there, much of it at GQ, firing most of the time. I remember three such times—one thirty hours, one twenty-six hours, and one sixteen hours. We fired at least every five minutes. As plotting room officer, I was the one pulling the trigger. After this was a trip north with the *Maddox* where the *Brush* hit the mine I mentioned earlier.

Then we had thirty days in dry dock in Sasebo. The *Brush* looked like a small boat in the bottom of the dry dock. The dry dock had been built for the *Yamato* and *Musashi*, the two largest battleships in the world. They were sunk in the battle off Samar in November 1944. During these days and following visits, I was able to help start an orphanage in Sasebo.

After the tour in dry dock, the *Brush* went to Yokosuka. While in Yokosuka, I looked up Bessie Dodds, the Canadian headmistress of a Bible school for women in Yokohama. Eighteen months later, we were married in Yokohama. That was sixty-four years ago, on April 7, 1952.

While the *Brush* was being patched up in Sasebo, I had requested a transfer to any combatant vessel remaining in the forward area. I got my orders to the *Brinkley Bass* (DD887) at Midway Island. I flew back to Japan and came aboard the *Bass* on January 1, 1951, by a high wire in the Sea of Japan right after the Hungnam evacuation.

I had one year at Monterey (1953–1954) in Command Communications then back to Japan on the staff of COM NAV FE in Yokosuka for a year, then most of another year with the Naval Security Group at Kamiseya in the Commander Carrier Division 5 staff.

My six years of active duty were very fruitful in evangelism. During them, I also married and had three children and experienced many exciting events in the Korean War. After leaving the Navy in November 1956, Bessie and I spent two years in Washington, D.C. In November 1958, we moved to Annapolis.

As a point of contact with midshipmen after leaving the Navy, I opened the Christian Bookshop for the Officers' Christian Fellowship on Maryland Avenue in Annapolis. I ran the Christian Bookshop for close to ten years while also traveling to other academies and military bases on the East Coast. It was during those years that I met the midshipmen whose stories you have just read.

I received Christ in October 1947. It has been 69 years of God's grace in many amazing ways.

Bessie and I have four children, fifteen grandchildren, and twenty-six great grandchildren. Our life together has been greatly blessed. Bessie died September 18, 2010.

If you would like to know more, visit the Community Christian Ministries website (ccmbooks.org) and my blog (rootsbytheriver.blogspot.com).

If one of these stories opened your eyes, you may realize that you are not a Christian. If you are not a Christian, then you have a nature that is prone to sin. You need a new nature, and you need to get rid of your old nature. This cannot be done by you. It can be done only by God.

Here is your part.

You need to want to be set free from the guilt and judgment for your sins and the power of sin.

You need to know that you are helpless in this want.

You need to know that being good and not being bad will not set you free, nor will any other means of self-effort.

You need to know that God has already accomplished this deliverance by sending the Lord Jesus to earth to die for the ungodly. "You see, at just the right time, when we were still powerless, Christ died for the ungodly" (Rom. 5:6).

Three days after His death for our sins, the Lord Jesus rose from the dead in order to make us righteous. "He was delivered over to death for our sins and was raised to life for our justification" (Rom. 4:25).

The Holy Spirit is now drawing you to turn from your sin, to call upon the Lord Jesus, trusting Him, His death, and His resurrection.

"That if you confess with your mouth, 'Jesus is Lord,' and believe in your heart that God raised him from the dead, you will be saved. For it is with your heart that you believe and are justified, and it is with your mouth that you confess and are saved" (Rom. 10:9).

"Now, brothers, I want to remind you of the gospel I preached to you, which you received and on which you have taken your stand. By this gospel you are saved, if you hold firmly to the word I preached to you. Otherwise, you have believed in vain. For what I received I passed on to you as of first importance: that Christ died for our sins according to the Scriptures, that he was buried, that he was raised on the third day according to the Scriptures, and that he appeared to Peter, and then to the Twelve" (1 Cor. 15:1-5).

Having called upon the Lord Jesus, thank Him for bringing you to the Father, for forgiving your sin, and for giving you everlasting life.

Now, in your joy of your forgiveness, tell someone about what God has done for you.

If you would like to know God truly, not just know about Him, and would like to be sure that you will go to Heaven when you die, please write to me. I will send you help in the form of books and booklets that will help you grow in the Christian life.

If this has interested you at all, I will be glad to correspond with you. If you are interested, but not in writing to me, I suggest that you read the Gospel of John and the first eight chapters of St. Paul's letter to the Romans. You may also call on a pastor or chaplain and talk to a close friend or relative whom you think is very clearly a Christian.

You can contact Jim Wilson by email at jimwilson27@frontier.com, postal mail at 114 S. Howard Street, Moscow, Idaho 83843, or telephone at (208) 882-4383.

APPENDIX A: OUTSPOKEN WITNESS

Alfred James Egerton, USNA Class of '62
(written by Jim Wilson)

I got to know A.J. in his Plebe year. He was from Texas and had come to the Academy to play football. I don't think he wound up playing. The summer after his Plebe year, his Youngster cruise was going through the St. Lawrence Seaway, which had just been opened.

A.J. had an infectious personality. I assumed he was a Christian and gave him a book on personal evangelism (*The Dynamic of Service*) which had been a great help to me. Several years later, A.J. told me that he had been saved reading that book.

On his senior cruise, he led a midshipman, class of '64, to Christ, who in turn led midshipmen to Christ up to the class of '68.

When A.J. was commissioned, he was assigned to a ship in the Mediterranean. It may not be their way today, but sailors used to keep a paperback book in their back pockets. In the Mediterranean, A.J. put 35 copies of Billy Graham's *Peace with God* in the back pockets of the sailors on his ship.

During his tour in the summer of 1963, A.J. fell over on the bridge. The doctor thought he had a psychological problem and sent him to the psychiatric ward in the Philadelphia Naval Hospital. The doctors there discovered that he had a massive malignant brain tumor. Surgery was performed, but the surgeon could not remove the entire tumor. I heard about it and also found out that the surgeon had not told A.J. that he had brain cancer.

I was at an OCF conference at Camp Wabanna when I made the decision to go to Philadelphia to tell A.J. about his cancer. Hal Guffey, USNA '55, accompanied me. We knew we would have to see the surgeon first. We did not know how to go about it. We had lunch in the cafeteria and prayed for guidance.

After lunch, we were walking down a corridor when a doctor in a white coat came around the corner, and we ran into each other. We both apologized, and he started to go on his way. I realized he looked familiar. I stopped and called, "Doctor!" He turned around. It was Joe Winston. His father-in-law, David Morken, had performed my wedding eleven years earlier in Yokohama, and I had been of some help to Joe and his wife when he was in medical school at Emery University.

He recognized me and said, "I know why you are here." He had been doing residency in the psych ward when A.J. was there. He said that he would go with us to see the surgeon. After much conversation with the three of us, the surgeon agreed to tell A.J. that he had terminal cancer.

A.J. met with the four of us, but the surgeon did not tell him about the cancer. He beat around the bush. Hal and I went back with A.J. to his room, and I told him. I said, "If you want the elders to pray for you, I will round them up in Philadelphia and come back here with them."

A.J. asked for time to pray about it. We came back. He answered that he did not want the elders to pray for him. He would rather go to be with Jesus. I thought he was dead wrong. He was only 23 years old. I argued with him until he finally consented to the prayer. I was wrong. I should not have pressured him.

A.J. was retired from the Navy with full disability. Instead of going home to Texas, he came to Annapolis and was a witness with me to the town.

I remember one incident when a woman came into the bookstore to see me. We were in the large room upstairs. I reached into my pocket for my New Testament. It wasn't there. While I was wondering where it was, I looked up, and there was a New Testament in the middle of the air coming towards me. A.J. had thrown one to me.

A.J. went to Texas for Christmas and died there on January 23, 1964.

APPENDIX B:
RUNNING THE RACE
FOR CHRIST

Following are some words from Otto Helweg, whose testimony appears on page 41, which he gave to Christian students about to enter university.*

* * *

But in your hearts reverence Christ as Lord.
Always be prepared to make a defense to any one who
calls you to account for the hope that is in you,
yet do it with gentleness and reverence.
(1 Peter 3:15 RSV)

*   Taken from two talks given at Logos High School, Moscow, Idaho, 18 April 2002; edited by Lisa Just for inclusion in *The USNA Twelve*.

Christian students can have their faith challenged regularly. Academia is not always a friendly place for Christians. In many university classes, Christianity has been dismissed as passé and is no longer considered intellectually credible. Statistics say that 60-70% of all high school students that were active in Sunday school lose their faith in college. When these students come to talk to me, I find that they are trying to answer postgraduate questions with junior-high theology. They have been lazy intellectually.

We live in an age of unbelief. This world does not believe in including God in daily life. Christians are also guilty of this. We think that our studies, our exams, are not of interest to God.* Have you ever said, "God, how are *we* going to do this?" Make Him a partner in your day-to-day life.

Can we create a system so perfect that no one would need to be good? The assumption of humanities and sociological studies is that we can. I enjoy technology and have devoted my profession to it. But when we deify technology, we empty our culture of substance and wisdom. Scientism only believes what has been proven and doubts all else. This creates specialists without spirit and sensualists without heart. It leads to ridiculous statements like, "Darwin made it possible to be an intellectually-fulfilled atheist."†

Mainstream humanities, social studies, and sciences don't believe in God anymore. Yet the founders of modern science were mostly Christians.

---

*   By the way, the tract by Brother Lawrence called *Practicing the Presence of God* should be required reading for any Christian.

†   Richard Dawkins, *The Blind Watchmaker*

Copernicus said the sun was the center of the universe, contrary to Aristotle, who believed that the earth was the center. In those days, going against Aristotle was like trying to deny the atomic theory of particles. Copernicus was very favorable to the Reformation.

Bacon, the father of the scientific method, thought that the workability of that method was one of the ways that God showed His logic in creation.

Galileo proposed the heliocentric solar system. Galileo is the favorite example of atheists, agnostics, and other anti-Christians for how anti-scientific the Christian faith is. If you study history, you will find that it was not the Church that was against Galileo, but professors. University professors at that time refused to look through any telescope that was pointed at the moon, because it showed craters and imperfections on the moon—and, according to them and Aristotle, there were no imperfections on the moon. They complained to the pope about Galileo. Galileo had many friends in the Church, including the influential Cardinal Baronius. Baronius said that God has given us two books—the book of His Word and the book of His works—and they don't contradict each other.

Kepler wanted to be a Lutheran minister, but he was such a genius with mathematics and astronomy that he was talked into pursuing those things instead. Our space program is based on his discoveries and computations. In his scientific writings, Kepler praises God on every other page. He became a scientist, not to gain fame, but to show that God had created a rational universe, which demonstrates that we worship a rational God.

Pascal is the father of modern hydrostatics, the father of probability theory, the father of modern mass transit, the father of modern French prose, and the father of modern Christian apologetics. He was one of the greatest scientific minds the world has ever seen. Pascal's genius was realized at an early age. When he was about eight, his father began schooling him in Greek, Hebrew, and Latin and moved to Paris in order that his son could have the very best education. When Pascal was nine or ten, his father went into his room and found that he had independently solved Euclid's thirty-second proposition. Pascal became a Christian. From the age of 18, he never experienced a day without intense pain. It became so bad that he could only imbibe liquids in small quantities, was unable to walk, and died at the age of 39. He wrote a tract about what a privilege it was to suffer as a Christian.

Newton thought his theological writings were much more important than his scientific writings.

Michael Faraday discovered electromagnetic induction. He was very much impressed with missions.

Maxwell discovered magnetic flux. Once in a sermon, Maxwell just read from the Bible because, as he said, "My words can add nothing to the Word of God."

These are the founders of modern science. Their goal was to bring glory to God from their discoveries.

So what happened? Darwin came along with *The Origin of Species*, and Huxley used it against Christianity. This happens regularly in the Church: God gives us a gift, then something attacks us. Rather than understanding the attack and countering it, we throw the baby out with the bathwater. Christians have developed an anti-scientific mentality since Darwin's time because we did not recognize the attack for what it was.

There are two lessons here. First, know what the Bible says, and don't make it say what it doesn't. Christians are often taught things that are extra-biblical. Read your entire Bible. Look at it as a target. In the center is the bull's eye—that is the Gospel. You don't need Greek or Hebrew to understand what it takes to know Jesus Christ in a personal way. But as you get out into the periphery of Revelation or the secondary doctrines, you have to do serious scholarship. You need to understand hermeneutics* when dealing with the esoteric issues.

Second, have a profound appreciation for God's creation. There is nothing to be afraid of here. God is the author of truth. We have His written Word, and we have His physical word in the world. When these things don't seem to jive, there are two possible problems. Either your interpretation is wrong, or the scientific theories are wrong. You need to be able to hold these two in suspension until you get them figured out. That is part of growing in Christian maturity. The Bible and science should be friends. If they're not, it is because we do not understand them or we are being deluded by Satan's lies.

God blessed Adam and Eve and sent them to be fruitful and multiply, to fill the earth and *subdue it*. What does that mean? God is telling us to find out how He did it! The scientific endeavor is part of fulfilling God's creation mandate.

---

* Hermeneutics is how to interpret the Bible.

We are fulfilling this basic command to subdue the earth as we exercise the talents He has given us. Find out how He did it.

I have told you about the men who founded modern science. Who is working in the field of science now?

Gerhard Dirks, "the father of the modern computer," was the head of research at IBM. He had an I.Q. of 208. They say Einstein's was 209. Gerhard Dirks became a Christian by trying to figure out what it would take to make a model of the human brain.

Francis Collins was head of the Human Genome Project and helped to map human DNA. His testimony was given in *MD* magazine, the official magazine for medical doctors. He became a Christian by reading C.S. Lewis.

Henry (Fritz) Schaefer has been nominated for the Nobel Prize five times. He is a chemistry professor from the University of Georgia and one of the most frequently cited scientists in the world. Every time he makes a discovery, he says, "So that's how God did it."

One cannot scientifically prove or disprove the existence of God. However, one can ask, "What does the character of nature suggest? Is it reasonable to believe that the universe just happened to be exactly right in so many ways?"

There are a number of fundamental universal constants (e.g. the speed of light) which must all be at specific values in order to have a universe that will support life. If any of them were just a little different, life as we know it could not exist. For example, if the strong force (which holds subatomic particles together) was increased by two percent, there would be no stable hydrogen and no hydrogen-containing compounds. If the ratio was reduced by five percent, there would be no stable hydrogen, no stable stars, and few (if any) elements besides hydrogen.

How long will the sun last? The energy of a star depends on the relative magnitude of the gravitational force, the electromagnetic force, and associated constants. The electromagnetic force is 10^{36} times stronger than the gravitational force. If the electromagnetic force were only 10^{30} stronger, stars would burn one million times faster, providing no long-term source of energy for the Earth.

There are approximately thirty-five conditions that must be just so for the universe to support life (for example, a stable source of energy, elemental diversity, matching of energy from the sun with chemical bonding energies, etc.). It is quite remarkable that they are all exactly what they need to be to provide this truly unique life-sustaining universe.

What does the second law of thermodynamics tell us? Basically, that everything runs downhill. Entropy is increasing. Nature is slowly destroying information. The universe is running down, and someday it will just be low-wave radiation. (Don't worry—that's going to be a long time yet.)

If nature *destroys* information, if the universe is slowly disintegrating over time, where did it all start? Where did this data, this information, this design come *from*? When the theory of the Big Bang first started, astrophysicists fought it tooth and nail because they knew that the implications of a *starting point* to the universe made their atheist worldview very, very questionable.

T.S. Eliot said, "The majority of mankind is lazy-minded, incurious, absorbed in vanities, and tepid in emotion, and is therefore incapable of either much doubt or much faith; and when the ordinary man calls himself a skeptic or unbeliever, that is ordinarily a simple pose, cloaking a disinclination to think anything out to a conclusion."

George Gaylord Simpson, a paleontologist and curator of the Museum of Comparative Zoology at Harvard: "It has become increasingly evident in our century that science is uncertain in its very nature; indeed, one thing that scientists can be quite certain is that they will not achieve a complete solution of any worthwhile problem."

Vannevar Bush, Chairman of the Board of MIT, the father of the analog computer: "Science proves nothing absolutely; on the most vital questions, it does not even produce evidence."

Albert Einstein: "The function of setting up goals and passing statements of value transcends the domain of science."

Francis Bacon: "Let no one think or maintain that a man can search too far or be too well-studied in the book of God's Word or in the book of God's works. We should not unwisely mingle or confound these learnings together."

"The fool says in his heart, 'There is no God'" (Psa. 14:1a RSV). "For what can be known about God is plain to them, because God has shown it to them. Ever since the creation of the world his invisible nature, namely, his eternal power and deity, has been clearly perceived in the things that have been made. So they are without excuse" (Rom. 1:19-20 RSV). "The heavens are telling the glory of God; and the firmament proclaims his handiwork" (Psa. 19:1 RSV).

I would like to leave you with the verse I started out with from 1 Peter: "But in your hearts reverence Christ as Lord. Always be prepared to make a defense to any one who calls you to account for the hope that is in you, yet do it with gentleness and reverence" (1 Pet. 3:15 RSV). As Christians, we debate from a position of strength. We know the Creator of the universe. We know absolute truth, even though we may not know all of the ramifications of it. I want to encourage you to grow in your intellectual understanding of God's great grace and His Kingdom.

My wife and I spent over ten years as missionaries in the Middle East. Our third year in Iran (before the Revolution), we had a very successful boys' club in a run-down building in Kermanshah, a city among the Kurds in western Iran. We had a ping-pong table, a shuffle-board, and a small volleyball court.

One time, a young high-schooler named Artisher came in and wanted to talk with me. It was very clear after a few sentences that he was not interested in Christianity at all. He was trying to convert me to communism. He and another friend of his had taken off the year before to go across the border into Iraq. They had gone to learn about communism and had come back to train other communists to start a revolution and overthrow the Shah.

It just so happened that I had a copy of the *Great Books of the Western World*, which has a section of Marx. It included the Communist Manifesto, which was banned in Iran. (I didn't know that at the time.) So we opened it up, and I translated it into Persian for him.

Artisher was dumbfounded. Almost all of the things that Marx claimed required a revolution had been accomplished in the United States without a revolution. This blew his theory of what was required to be a good communist. He said, "Well, what do Christians have to say?"

We started looking at the Bible. He said, "Wait a minute. I know that the Bible predicts the coming of Mohammed. So there's no way that you can convince me that Jesus was anything other than a prophet." (Muslims believe that when Christ talked about the Comforter, He was prophesying the coming of Mohammed.)

We opened up to John where it says, "the Comforter, the Holy Spirit" (John 14:26). Artisher was amazed. That one verse completely changed his mind, and he asked me about becoming a Christian.

I didn't believe that he was serious. For a Muslim to become a Christian is pretty rare. In our six and a half years in Iran, we could probably count the number of converts on one hand. And they thought we were having a revival!

He came back the next day and said, "I've asked Jesus to come into my life."

Artisher was a natural leader, one of the top academic students in a city of about 200,000 people. He always had six to eight guys around him. As soon as he became a Christian, his friends left. He had lived in the home of his widowed mother and older brother, and they kicked him out. The only place he could stay was in the poorest section of the city with another widow and a friend—the three of them in one room. Their only running water was a community faucet. There were no internal sanitation facilities at all. He really had nothing.

Although my wife and I were missionaries, I was loaned to the Ministry of Water and Power as an engineer to help with government projects, and I was able to get Artisher a job with an American company that was installing a satellite system for the Iranian government.

He started out this job on a remote site. Several days later, at three o'clock in the morning, there was a pounding on our door. I went, and there was Artisher, cut and bloody. The other workers had attacked him on the site and tried to kill him. He managed to get away and ran about two miles to the nearest road, but nobody would pick him up. He finally stood in front of a semi-truck. The driver stopped and brought him into the city. We took him to the emergency room and got him patched up.

From that point on, Artisher was a center of evangelism in that city. You could always find him on a street corner with a crowd around him.

"If you have raced with men on foot, and they have wearied you, how will you compete with horses? And if in a safe land you fall down, how will you do in the jungle of the Jordan?" (Jer. 12:5 RSV). More than half of high-schoolers who consistently attend Sunday school and church lose their faith in college. If in a safe land you fall down, you are going to have a tough time in the jungle of the Jordan. What I'd like to encourage you to do in college is to grow in your faith and also to look beyond that to the direction God would have you take with your life.

When Christian university students come to my office, they think the two most important decisions they have to make are 1) Who should I marry? and 2) What should my profession be? They are really surprised when I tell them, "Look. These are certainly important questions, but in God's economy, they are relatively trivial. The thing that is most important to God is not what you are going to do three, five, or seven years from now, but what you are going to do *today*."

Consider a missile laser guidance system. When the guidance system is turned on, the missile can start off in almost any direction, and it will still come back on course and find the target. The Holy Spirit is our guidance system. If that is kept finely tuned, we will find God's will in our lives. This fine-tuning is done in meeting with the Lord: your daily prayer, your study of the Word. Doing these things day after day, week after week, year after year, might seem rather mundane. But it is absolutely critical to maintaining your direction on the beam of God's will.

I have three suggestions for you. Number one: work to discover what your calling is. Everybody has a talent—Christians and non-Christians. Some have a talent for being a teacher, some scientists, some engineers, some educators, some mechanics, etc. This is something God has given to you. It is in your genetic makeup and probably also in your upbringing. There is also another thing which the Bible calls spiritual gifts (see 1 Corinthians, Romans, and Ephesians). These are only given to Christians, and they are given to build up the body of Christ.

If you have several talents, it may be tough to know what to study in college. That's okay. The main thing is to be tuned in to what the Lord wants you to do. He may direct you to places that you cannot foresee.

Number two: be open to adopting a country. There are exciting things going on in the world. It's one thing to learn the language; it's another thing to learn the culture. In the incarnation, God enculturated Himself into our time/space continuum. In a sense, that is what a Christian needs to do in another country. Right now, ninety percent of the resources of Christianity are concentrated in about ten percent of the world. It ought to be the other way around. If you are willing to listen to God's call, think about countries. If there is one that the Lord lays on your heart, pray about it. Get to know it. Maybe even visit it.

Number three: investigate opportunities to serve the Lord overseas. Read the exciting stories of pioneer missionaries like William Carey, Samuel Zwemer, John Wesley, and others who have gone out to spread the Gospel.

In 1910, 1,400 Christians came together in Edinburgh, Scotland, for the World Missionary Conference. Only eighteen of the attendees were from non-western countries; none were from Africa. The world is different today. It is probable that last Sunday more believers attended church in China than in all of so-called "Christian" Europe. Last Sunday, more Anglicans attended church in Egypt, Kenya, South Africa, Tanzania, and Uganda than did Anglicans in Britain and Episcopalians in the United States combined. Last Sunday, more Presbyterians were at church in Ghana than in Scotland, the home of Presbyterianism. Last Sunday, the churches with the largest attendance in England and France had mostly black congregations. The pastor of the Yoido Full Gospel Church in Seoul, South Korea, is a friend of mine. The Yoido Full Gospel Church is currently holding around-the-clock prayer meetings averaging several thousand people.* Their church is growing so fast that they have asked the members not to come on Sunday mornings so the seekers are able to get in. Now that, friends, is exciting.

Find out where the Holy Spirit is working and get on board. Unless it's in the Muslim world, the country you wind up in will probably have Christians. Even if you go overseas as a professional and not as a missionary, you can use the talents and spiritual gifts that God has given you to assist the Christians in that country to spread the Gospel. It may not be as exciting as putting on a pith helmet and wading through the jungles of Africa, but it's much, much more effective.

For example, as an engineer in Iran, I was able to bring safe drinking water to people that otherwise would have died. The number-one cause of death in developing countries is dysentery due to impure water. Engineers can solve this. The number-one cause of poverty in developing countries is lack of education. If you are educated, you can solve that. (Almost anyone can learn to teach English as a foreign language.) The number-one cause of economic stagnation is lack of business training. Someone with a business major can solve that. The number-one cause of technological backwardness is lack of technical training. A mechanic can solve that.

Be sure that what you are doing is unto the Lord in cooperation with the Christian church. Show the people around

* In April 2002

you that the Gospel affects their lives. You will have the dual privilege of seeing people who may otherwise die, live—and not only live physically, but live spiritually. That is much more exciting to me than earning a lot of money in the United States, because it is laying up treasure in heaven.

Of course, not everyone should go overseas. Many of you are called to serve in the United States. There is a great lack of belief here, and we should be concerned with evangelism in our own country and among our own families and neighbors. You need wisdom and God's guidance to keep you from going to the wrong places.

God may call you to go to the Muslim world; and let me tell you, it is tough. You are like the point person in a jungle patrol. Those are the ones who run into the booby traps and get picked off by snipers. There are times when your prayers seem to bounce off the ceiling, and you wonder, "How come the Lord isn't taking care of this?"

There's a very interesting verse in the book of Daniel. Daniel was praying and fasting. After three weeks, the Lord sent a messenger:

> Fear not, Daniel, for from the first day that you set your mind to understand and humbled yourself before your God, your words have been heard, and I have come because of your words. The prince of the kingdom of Persia withstood me twenty-one days; but Michael, one of the chief princes, came to help me, so I left him there with the prince of the kingdom of Persia and came to make you understand what is to befall your people in the latter days. For the vision is for days yet to come. (Dan. 10:12-14 RSV)

Basically, the angel said, "It isn't that we're hard of hearing up here. We heard your prayers from the very first day, but Satan contended against us until God sent Michael to neutralize him so that the Word could go forth." We have been singularly unsuccessful in penetrating the Muslim world. It is demonic. There is tremendous warfare there. God will have send someone to neutralize the power of Islam.

Is there any danger in going to places to like that as a missionary? Yes. Many Christians have been put in jail or killed because of their faith in recent years. The level of danger depends on the country. In Saudi Arabia, it is illegal for citizens to be Christian. Just before I went there, half a dozen Americans were deported for holding a Bible study in their home. Consequently, when I arrived I didn't start preaching on the street corner and passing out tracts.

I went to Saudi Arabia to establish a water research center as a tent-making missionary. (You can't be a professional missionary in Saudi Arabia.) I wanted to take twenty Arabic New Testaments with me. I put all my books into five-kilo packages that could be sent over much less expensively. But I had one large box that I planned to put the Bibles in the center of. If you are with the State Department, as I was, customs does not look through your things very carefully, so this was the safest place for them.

When we got to Saudi Arabia, our big box came, and we opened it up—no New Testaments. We panicked. The box had been opened, but it didn't look like anyone had gone through it. If they had found those Bibles, we would have been kicked out of the country in a nanosecond.

I went to my office at the King Faisal University. It was full of the five-kilo packages. All had been opened and searched except three. Those three contained the Arabic New Testaments. I don't like to use the word "miracle" flippantly, but God really protected us there. We were able to use those New Testaments to share the Gospel unobtrusively.

It is one thing to share the Gospel in the United States and know that the person who is converted has a good environment to grow in and learn about the Lord. When you share the Gospel with someone for whom accepting the Lord means being in danger of their lives and getting kicked out of their family, it causes you to pause. You can't just send them to the wolves. You need to be there for them after their conversion.

While we were in Saudi Arabia, we went scuba diving in the Persian Gulf (or the Arabian Gulf, depending which side you're on), and we saw seahorses. Seahorses are really, really clever. I had only seen them in aquariums before. They reminded me of the story of Freddie.

Freddie was a teenage seahorse, and he wanted to go out and seek his fortune. He had the undersea monetary means—six pieces of eight. He started out and ran into a squid.

The squid said, "Hey Freddie, where are you going?"

Freddie said, "I'm going out to seek my fortune."

The squid said, "This is a pretty competitive world. I'll tell you what I'm going to do. For two pieces of eight, I can sell you an outboard motor that will make you go fifty percent faster."

Freddie thought that was a pretty good deal. He forked over two pieces of eight, strapped on the outboard motor, and, sure enough, he went fifty percent faster.

He hadn't traveled very far when he met a cod. The cod said, "Hey Freddie, where are you going?"

Freddie said, "I'm out to seek my fortune."

The cod said, "It's pretty brutal out here. I'm going to give you a great bargain. I will sell you a jet assist that will double your speed. Two pieces of eight."

Freddie thought, "That's a great deal." So he forked over two pieces of eight, strapped on the jet, and sure enough, he doubled his speed.

Well, he was going pretty fast and ran into a shark. The shark said, "Freddie, where are you going?"

Freddie said, "I'm going to seek my fortune."

The shark said, "That's very impressive. I'll tell you what I'm going to do. For two pieces of eight, I will tell you where the fortune is."

"Yeah? Well, that's fantastic! I don't need pieces of eight if I find my fortune." And he forked it over to the shark.

The shark opened his mouth and motioned inside. Freddie went in, and of course that's the end of the story.

If you don't know where you're going, it doesn't make any difference how fast you travel. Continually bring these questions before the Lord: Where do You want me to go? What do You want me to do? What are the talents You have given to me? What are the spiritual gifts You have given me, and how can I use them to build up the body of Christ? Make this a matter of daily prayer. Be sensitive to the leading of the Spirit. Remember Jeremiah: If you have raced with men, and they have wearied you, how will you compete with horses? If in a safe land you fall down, how will you do in the jungle of the Jordan?

If you are currently in the United States and have access to a good church community, you are in a tremendous environment. You have the opportunity to grow spiritually. Don't take it for granted. Be like a sponge—soak up not just the intellectual but the spiritual knowledge you have access to. I trust the Lord is going to use you greatly for His kingdom.